The Vedic Dharma

Explorations in the Vedic Natural Order (Rta)

The Secret History of the Vedas, Volume I

James Kalomiris

BALBOA.PRESS
A DIVISION OF HAY HOUSE

Balboa Press books may be ordered through booksellers or by contacting:

Balboa Press
A Division of Hay House
1663 Liberty Drive
Bloomington, IN 47403
www.balboapress.com
844-682-1282

Because of the dynamic nature of the Internet, any web addresses or links contained in this book may have changed since publication and may no longer be valid. The views expressed in this work are solely those of the author and do not necessarily reflect the views of the publisher, and the publisher hereby disclaims any responsibility for them.

The author of this book does not dispense medical advice or prescribe the use of any technique as a form of treatment for physical, emotional, or medical problems without the advice of a physician, either directly or indirectly. The intent of the author is only to offer information of a general nature to help you in your quest for emotional and spiritual well-being. In the event you use any of the information in this book for yourself, which is your constitutional right, the author and the publisher assume no responsibility for your actions.

Any people depicted in stock imagery provided by Getty Images are models, and such images are being used for illustrative purposes only.
Certain stock imagery © Getty Images.

Print information available on the last page.

ISBN: 978-1-9822-2559-9 (sc)
ISBN: 978-1-9822-2560-5 (e)

Balboa Press rev. date: 10/14/2020

DEDICATION

To all those who provided their love and support over the years, but especially to my children, Kelley and Alex, to Niki, my Bright Star, and to Mary Murphy, my yogini, who so long ago started my journey through the Vedas.

CONTENTS

THE SECRET HISTORY OF THE VEDAS

This volume is the first installment in a new series on the Rig Veda. That series is The Secret History of the Vedas. The purpose of this series, The Secret History of the Vedas, is to unravel and discover the true meaning of the Vedic deities and to reveal the hidden meaning of the Vedas. While the meaning of the Vedas will perhaps be forever beyond the grasp of the humans and worshipers alike, somewhere, deeply embedded in the rcs (mantras) of the Rg Veda, those secrets are there waiting to be uncovered. This series reveals the hidden meaning of the Rg Veda, reassembled from portions of the Vedas — the Rg Veda SamaVeda, Yajur Veda, and AtharvaVeda — as well as the Brahmanas, Upanishads, shastras, and other Vedic and Hindu writings. This series is the key that unlocks the secrets of the Vedas.

Shrouded in great, immeasurable, antiquity, the Vedas are capable of many interpretations. The Rig Veda — and all the Vedas — may be read as mythology, as history, as simple story-telling or simply as a book of poetry. But there is a secret, deeper, meaning. Arriving at this meaning, however, can be very problematic. Reading the Rg Veda in translation often makes little sense, especially if read from the Victorian era translations. Even when considered as simple mythological stories and when reading the Vedas in translations, one cannot help but notice patterns of themes and characters and thereby perceive an inner grandeur and depth of meaning. If the stanzas and rcs (mantras) are properly decoded, and the proper passwords understood, the Vedas come alive and reveal a vast repository of occult knowledge concerning the nature of existence, divinity, and everything within. It is a "Secret History" not only because of the occult nature of this knowledge but because so few understand the language and passwords of the Vedas to dig deeper into its meaning. Armed with knowledge of the passwords used in the Vedas and with a proper interpretation, this hidden meaning, even when read in English translation, is intelligible and is ready to be unlocked. This is the purpose of this series and of the present volume.

INTRODUCTION

"The words have different meanings."
Pink Floyd, Piper at the Gates of Dawn.

This book is a systematic treatment of an important concept which pervades the Rg Veda, *rta*. In this present book *Rta* will go by different names. *Rta* will be called the Natural Order, the Cosmic Natural Order, the Universal Order the dynamic cosmic order, or any derivation therein. There are many synonyms for the Natural Order but they all refer to one umbrella concept: The Vedic dharma.

Explaining *Rta* necessarily includes an examination of the Vedic deities. The great, and yet untold, story of the Vedic deities is their identification with the active, subtle and natural forces in the universe we all encounter every day. Attempts have been made in the past to equate the Vedic deities as natural phenomena, mental states, or spiritual values. In reality, the Vedic deities are all these, and more. The Vedic pantheon of deities — Agni, Indra, Soma and the others — represent these forces encountered every day, and the forces which underpin those natural phenomena, mental states, or spiritual values. When it is said that the Vedic deities simply represent natural phenomena, mental states, or spiritual values, their visceral, primeval nature is ignored. This is where *rta*, the Vedic dharma, comes in.

This book is about the Vedic dharma, *rta*. *Rta* is a bedrock principle. *Rta*, or the Vedic dharma — the Natural Order — serves as both an umbrella sheltering the other Vedic forces and principles and at the same time is that force and principle itself. As is their wont, the several other Vedic deities are the administrators of *rta*, the Natural Order, and at the

1

same time powered by that Natural Order. This present book attempts to unravel, deconstruct and rearraign the relationship between *rta*, the Vedic dharma, and the Vedic forces which populate that order. The scope of this text is limited to the principles mentioned in the Asyavamasya Sukta, a textbook explaining the nature of *rta*, the Vedic dharma, and all other Vedic and Hindu resources.

Every age has its own Zeitgeist. Unlike our present age, the Kali Yuga, which is concerned with materialism and consumerism, early ages were concerned with the investigation of the Vedic dharma which pervades and runs this material world and how life may proceed in harmony with that order. This concern was the preoccupation of the early philosophers and seers. These thinkers and Rishiis reduced these revelations as best as could be communicated:

- In the I Ching which was concerned with this dynamic cosmic order. This inscrutable scripture interpreted and explained the dynamic cosmic order (*rta*) in terms of its hexagrams. The I Ching explained pictorially what the Rg Veda explained in writing with symbols.
- By Heraclitus who spoke of the Logos, which is the link between rational discourse and the world's rational structure.
- By the Stoics, who focused their philosophical discussions about the Logos.

These doctrines have their origin in the Vedic dharma. That common thread is the primordial essence and fundamental nature in the universe, and in ages past it was the worshiper's mission to discover that primordial essence, to live in accordance with that essence, to be inspired and informed by that essence, thereby molding the worshiper's life accordingly.

In the Vedic world that concern decreased considerably with the appearance of the Upanishads. Thereafter, liberation was not achieved by living in accordance with the Natural Order, but with the identification with Atman, the Absolute Self. As a unitary concept, *rta*, the Vedic dharma, as a concept, was discarded to give meaning to Brahman. Elsewhere, the emphasis in the Common Era moved further away from the desire to discover and live in accordance with the Natural Order. With the advent of the Christian Era, this tradition with Vedic dharma, of the Natural Order, waned. Concern for the dynamic cosmic order was eliminated at least in the Western world. Liberation ceased to be the worshiper's goal. Salvation became the goal, and Salvation was achieved as the result of an act of Grace. Part of the reason for this is that the Logos is by its nature an undefined term, and except for generalized definitions, spoken of in symbols and imagery. The Natural Order was not easily understood, and because it was not understood, not used. Emphasis on living in accordance with the Natural Order, let alone discovering what that Natural Order was, seemed less and less important.

Enter the Asyavamasya Sukta, Rig Veda. The Asyavamasya Sukta is group of rcs, or mantras, verses, in the Rg Veda. These rcs or verses are found in Sukta 164 of the First Mandala. The Asyavamasya Sukta contains the major themes operating within the Natural Order (*rta*) in its rcs (mantras) and stanzas. These themes are repeated, expanded, and referenced throughout the Rg Veda and the other Vedas, and throughout later Hindu thought and philosophy. This present volume is a running commentary on each stanza of the Asyavamasya Sukta.

I can see the question mark over your head. What is the Asyavamasya Sukta? If the average general reader has heard of any Sukta in the Rig Veda, it's been the Purusa Sukta, or, perhaps the Nasadiya Sukta. The Asyavamasya Sukta, however, is equally important.

The Asyavamasya Sukta, RV 1.164, is an explanation of the creation and establishment of *rta*, the Universal, natural and dynamic order which regulates the universe — the Vedic dharma. *Rta*, the Vedic dharma, is not limited to the material universe we all live in but includes the unseen engine which runs the material world. The Asyavamasya Sukta is a systematic treatment of Vedic dharma. The Asyavamasya Sukta describes the Vedic divine forces at work in the natural cosmic order of things (*rta*), its constituent elements, and how those principles may be applied in the life of the worshiper. The Asyavamasya Sukta describes the various parts which run this marvelous machine, our universe, and relationship of these parts with the divine Vedic forces (deities) which they operate. In this function the Asyavamasya Sukta is a repository of the deepest knowledge of the inner mechanics of the universe and the inner workings of the cosmic order (*rta*). For example, it explains and describes the establishment of the cosmic order (*rta*) and the relationship of *Rta* with the earth and the Sun.

The Asyavamasya Sukta vacillates between serving as this repository of scientific knowledge and alternating into deep philosophical discussions explaining, in its coded language, the foundations of the universe.

The Asyavamasya Sukta does not concern itself with mere philosophical, religious or mystical musings. The worshiper, the religious seeker, is its guest as the sukta explores the boundaries of the dynamic cosmic order and how this marvelous structure applies to and assists the worshiper to achieve liberation and salvation. In this quest at times it achieves the poignancy of the Divine Comedy, the only difference being is that instead of the worshiper is being guided by Virgil; the dynamic cosmic order (*rta*) is the guide, as revealed to the Rishii Dirghatama. The Vedas speak of *rta*, the Vedic Dharma, but does not define it. The concepts are clothed in veiled, mystic language. Much like the Dao, it is a concept subsumed in the essence of everything, an elusive concept which defies definition. There are contours to *rta*, which this chapter seeks to chart for the benefit of the general reader or the worshiper while traveling the Vedic path to liberation and salvation.

Why should the worshiper care? To achieve liberation to transcend the world the worshiper must know its boundaries. When the "first born of *rta*," the power and force of the Vedic gods, reaches the worshiper, it is hoped the worshiper will grasp its meaning. The hope and expectation are that this understanding will aid the worshiper while on the Vedic path of salvation and liberation.

In a scripture as preoccupied so much with *Rta* (dharma) — the dynamic, divine order — piecing together a coherent statement is like reassembling an immense jig saw puzzle. The mantras of the Vedas defy a coherent message. Like nearly all the other Suktas and mantras and rcs of the Veda, the meaning of the words is shrouded in obscure symbols. Recourse to that coherent message requires not simply reading the Vedas. One must know the user names and passwords. From the very beginning it was said that the Vedas love being obtuse. The same is true of the Asyavamasya Sukta. Obscurity is name of the game. Finding the next explanatory piece to an obscure passage or word may be found elsewhere in a Brahmana or an Aranyaka. However, once one recognizes the passwords and understands the coded language, its meaning becomes clear.

This book originates from a much larger exposition of the Vedas. Having seen the complete treatise, taken was unmanageable, I broke the larger work into smaller sections. What better starting place but to discuss the concept of *rta*, the Vedic dharma. I found the available literature to be unsatisfactory. At worst, other texts were no better than glossaries, citing the text of the Asyavamasya Sukta, verse to verse, and providing only a translation of the words contained therein. At best, other texts merely scratched the surface. There was no book which explained what *Rta* really was, deep down, and the role it played in the Vedas.

What follows does not pretend to give the definitive interpretation of this Sukta. This is merely a "modest interpretation." A definitive interpretation by any one person explaining *Rta* in all its contexts and applications is not possible. In the final analysis, this author will paraphrase RV 1.164.18 in saying "Who can really say they understand the Asyavamasya Sukta?" The only genuine answer is "no one." The "real" interpretation of the Veda is anyone's guess.

Instead, what follows is this modest interpretation, an attempt to explain this riddle and present it in a cogent, coherent fashion. It provides one possible interpretation of what the Sukta has to say about the Vedic dharma (*rta*). It is an introduction of the different aspects of the Vedic dharma, *rta*. It also treats the varied aspects of the Vedic dharma: The Vedic deities, their powers, their application to our world, the very structure of physical reality. This knowledge is exactly what is needed by the worshiper while on the path to salvation and liberation. If the worshiper is to be liberated from the maya in this world, the worshiper must first understand the world's boundaries. It is not a traditional look at rta, otherwise known herein as the Natural Order or the Vedic dharma, or of any Vedic subject. It is an idiosyncratic view but one which explains the Vedic corpus in an integrated, truly wholistic manner.

Whenever possible, assertions about this Natural Order are supported by doctrinal references. It is the author's sincere hope that you, dear Reader, will not be intimidated by thecitations. The presence of the footnotes in this text are not meant to annoy or vex you. They are included as much for the benefit for those curious for additional knowledge and reference, as much as it is for the author's own assurance that he is not falling into error. If the interpretation is incorrect, outlandish, audacious, unfounded, unorthodox, or simply mistaken, the fault lies not in the Vedas, or in the rcs in this marvelous, moving, piece of wisdom, but belongs solely to the author.

WHAT IS THE VEDIC DHARMA?

**"[God] created human beings and let them develop
according to the internal laws that he gave to each
one so they would reach their fulfillment."**

Pope Francis, reported on October 28, 2014.

In the movie American Gangster, a mafia boss bemoans to the Denzel
Washington character, "More important than any one man's life is Order."
What is that "Order," the Dharma in the Rg Veda?

In our present Kali Yuga, at least in the Western World, we are guided
by the principles Western Liberalism articulated in and discovered during
the Enlightenment period. According to those principles, the Individual
and individual rights are elevated such that the rights of the Individual
are paramount. Continental philosophers call the Individual person the
"Subject," and it is emphasized to the exclusion of all else. It is tempting
to think that this Subject is an offshoot of the Self in Hindu thought,
but that is not the case. In Classical Vedanta the Absolute Self is the
Subject which superimposes its Consciousness on the thinking, perceiving
individual. It, the Absolute Self, is the witnessing Subject, not the person.
In Western Liberalism, the "Subject" is the perceiving organism, that
entity which is identified as the Object in Classical Vedanta, that upon
which the Self superimposes consciousness. Western Liberalism thereby
elevates the Object and transforms it to the Subject. It is no surprise to
see the interminable Continental ruminations about "the Subject." These
ruminations resemble a dog chasing its tail. This slavish pandering to

the Subject creates a myopia to such a great degree that the very term, "Enlightenment," becomes an oxymoron, devoid and bereft of meaning. This is one of the sources of all the confusion and turmoil in our Kali Yuga.

In bygone eras, however, the Zeitgeist contemporaneous to the Vedas sought to discover the very rhythm of the greater cosmos which envelopes the material world and integrate that rhythm in harmony with everyday life. Salvation and liberation are obtained for those who lived in harmony with this greater rhythm. In Ancient Egypt that greater rhythm was called the Law; in Ancient China, the Dao; to the ancient Greeks, Heraclitus, Plato, and the Stoics, Logos. In the Indus Valley this natural rhythm, or order, of the universe was called *rta*, the Vedic dharma.

As the quotation from Pope Francis indicates, *Rta* is closely tied with the internal laws of that greater cosmos. These laws are not limited to laws relating the mechanical operation of the world as discovered by modern physics. The laws of *rta*, the Natural Order, the Vedic dharma, implicate the subtle laws of the consciousness that guides those mechanical laws and of all sentient beings. (RV 1.145.5; 4.3.4; 4.16.11; 5.3.9; 7.85.4.)

Rta is the dynamic, natural, and cosmic order of things and encompasses both the mechanical and subtle laws of the universe. It is the Universal Order. It is the Dao. It is also the principal topic of concern in the Rg Veda. However, in a manner typical for the Rishiis of the Rg Veda, musings, explanations, principles, or examples of the inner workings of *Rta* were explained in symbols, shrouded in heavily coded, obscure language.

The Asyavamasya Sukta, found in Sukta 164 of the First Mandala of the Rg Veda, perhaps the most obscure of all passages in the Vedas, and yet is the most systematic to describe the inner components of the Vedic version of the Vedic Dharma, *rta*, the natural cosmic order. *Rta* is the Vedic dharma. *Rta* is a concept which predominates the Rg Veda. Both *Rta* and the Dharma embrace the same values and have the same aims. The Vedic dharma is part science, describing the macrocosmic universe; it is part physics, explaining the mechanics of the universe; part philosophy, guiding the worshiper through the inner structure and workings of the universe; and part religion providing the worshiper with the means for salvation and liberation.

The Vedas speak of *rta*, the Vedic dharma, but do not define it very well. Much like the Tao, it is a concept subsumed in the essence of everything, an elusive concept which defies a hard and fast definition. Much is assumed and left unsaid. According to the Vedic world everything is informed by and follows *rta*. *Rta* defies an easy explanation. Like any other issue of Vedic interpretation, there is no single exposition defining this important issue. Instead, the worshiper is forced to engage in a complex jigsaw puzzle approach, picking a selection from a Brahmana, choosing a passage from an Upanishad there, other rcs or a saman elsewhere or from other divergent sources, only to reassemble these pieces into some coherent discourse. This tract will seek to navigate the worshiper through the various scriptures who travels on the Vedic path to liberation and salvation.

In the Vedas and Brahmans, this dynamic cosmic order was a real concern. *Rta* is a concept of great importance to the ideology in the Veda, if not the Hindu world, yet is a concept which is the most difficult for the Western mind to fully comprehend. Given its ubiquity in the Vedas, the inherent inadequacy of the English language to a translate the full meaning of *rta*, and the centrality of the concept, the Vedas do not give a coherent explanation of *Rta* or explain *Rta* other in simile, as an association of the Vedic deities who are the dynamic forces operating in the material world and are born from and then supervise the observance of the Natural Order.

Yet the concept itself is not unknown to Western thought. *Rta* is a concept not easily rendered in a single English word. Thus, in translation, the cosmic order (*rta*) is translated as "sacrifice" or as the "cosmic" or "transcendent" order of things, or the "divine law," barely scratching the surface. Indeed, philosophically, the closest equivalent is the doctrine of natural law of Hobbes, or *Logos* of the Heraclitus. *Rta* is this and more. Where the focus of Hobbes' natural laws is the material world, *Rta* originates in the transcendent world surpassing even the divinities and thereby governs this material world.

Rta is derived from the root, *r* meaning *gati*, or motion, or "to go, move, rise, tend up-wards." This understanding is best demonstrated in relation to the structure of Vedic cosmology. According to this structure of the cosmos, there are the three higher worlds: the *tridhataaltu*, or *mahih*, the Macrocosm, consisting of *Satyam*, Absolute Being, or Truth; *Cittam*, Conscious Force; and *Ananda*, Bliss. There are the three lower worlds, *Vyarhrta*, of the Microcosm, consisting of *Svar*, the Supermind; the *Antariksha*, or *bhuvah*, consisting of *prana*, or the Life-Force; and the bhuh, consisting of *Prakrti*, earth, matter. Svar, interpreted as the Sun-World, or the World of Light, binds the higher and lower worlds and acts as the focal point gaining entry to the one from the other. *Rta* "rises" or "moves upwards," above these three worlds, consists of the Empyrean, at the same time providing the foundation for all that exists below.

The quotation from Pope Francis is as close to the meaning of *Rta* as any the English language. *Rta* includes the internal laws of the universe. It also informs the internal laws which govern the conduct of sentient beings. Most dictionaries translate *Rta* in many ways. The available translations render *Rta* in many ways which include "truth," "truth in movement," which is distinguished from "eternal law," "sacrifice," "divine orders," "eternal law," "sacrifice," "divine orders," "holy rite," and many others.

Whatever its translation, there is no adequate single English word for *rta*. In classical philosophy the closest equivalent would be the Empyrean, that realm of pure fire and light which transcends the seven levels of existence. Throughout the ages, this world has acquired different names to different doctrines. To the Platonists, this realm was the Forms or the Good; to the Neo-Platonists, it was the One; Christianity supplanted both these concepts into God or the Trinity. Modernly, it has no name, while the concept remains. For the purposes of this examination, the *Rta* is best explained in Western terms as "Metaphysics." Given its wide breadth of wisdom in the Rg Veda, it is difficult to single out one concept which is the object of that wisdom. If it were possible to name one focus of the Rg Veda, that concept would be *Rta*, the Natural Order, i.e., dharma.

Rta in the Rg Veda operates on many levels:

- On a physical level, it defines the inner structure of the material world.
- On a cosmic level *Rta* regulates the dynamics of nature. If the Vedic deities are divine dynamic forces, *Rta* is the divine dynamism and essence from which these forces are empowered. If not referred by name, *Rta* will be discussed in this book as the "divine dynamism and essence" of the cosmos.

- On a microcosmic level, *Rta* is the active principle that regulates time and the temporal sequence of everyday life and maintains the balance between the cosmic and microcosmic levels.
- On a macrocosmic level, *Rta* establishes the cosmologic structure of the universe, from the smallest particle to the entire cosmos.
- On a religious level *Rta* informs the operation of the microcosm and macrocosm as they are reflected in the sacrificial rite. This representation is the primary purpose of the sacrifice: to symbolize the creation, maintenance, dissolution and subsequent revitalization of the cosmos, and apply these principles to the worshiper.

The Veda can be viewed as a panegyric to Vedic dharma. Again, given its multi-faceted meaning, there are a vast number of derivations and word cognates, signifying a different aspect of the Natural Order, which is testament to the preeminence of *rta*, dharma, in the Veda. From *Rta* is derived several words which are essential to the understanding of the Vedas, such as *ghrta*, clarified butter, and *a/mRta*, immortality. Here are others:

- Rtu, the regular sequencing of the temporal order. (RV 1.15.4; 1.49.3; 1.84.18; 1.95.3; 1.162.19; 3.47.2; 4.34.2; 5.32.2; 10.2.1; 10.7.6; 10.18.5; 10.26.1; 10.85.18.)
- Rtuna, the temporal sequence of the manifest world. (RV 1.51.1; 1.5.2; 1.5.3. 1.5.4; 1.15.5; 1.15.6 1.15.9; 1.15.10; 1.15.11; 1.15.20; 1.49.3; 2.37.6; 1.84.18; 1.95.4; 1.162.4.)
- rtena, according to the eternal aspect of the cosmic order, pursuant to the sequential order of the material world. (RV 1.23.5; 1.133.1; 1.152.1; 1.185.6; 2.27.8; 3.4.5; 3.5.3; 3.31.9. 21; 4.3.9, 10; 4.23.9; 4.42.4; 5.1.7; 5.12.3; 5.15.2; 5.62.1; 5.63.7; 5.68.4; 5.80.1; 6.68.2; 7.34.7.56.12; 7.8.86.5; 9.80.8; 9.108.8; 10.12.1, 2; 19,62.2, 3; 10.108.11; 10.109.1; 10.123.4, 5; 10.139.4.)
- Rtutha. (RV 1.164.19; 1.164.44; 1.70.5; 2.3.7; 2..431; 5.32.12; 6.9.3; 6.18.3; 6.62.9; 8.13.19; 8.44.8; 9.97.12; 10.28.5; 10.40.4; 10.85.16; 10.98.11; 10.110.10; 10.131.3.)

- rtavam, possessed of *rta*. (RV 1.77.1; 1.22.9; 2.24.7; 2.27.7; 2.35.8; 3.2.13; 3.13.2; 3.20.4; 3.53.8; 3.54.12; 3.56.8; 4.1.2; 4.2.1; 4.6.5; 4.7.3, 7; 4.38.7; 5.1.8; 5.25.1; 5.65.2; 5.67.4; 6.12.1; 6.73.1; 7.3.1; 7.7.4; 7.39.7; 7.40.7; 7.61.2; 7.62.3; 7.66.13; 7.87.3; 8.25.1, 4, 7, 8; 8.75.3; 9.96.13; 9.97.48; 10.2.1; 10.6.2; 10.7.4; 10.140.6; 10.154.4; 10.168.3.)
- rtayu, observance of *rta*. (RV 1.34.10; 1.121.4; 1.137.2; 1.151.3, 6; 1.153.3; 4.3.8; 4.23.10; 5.20.4; 9.17.8; 9.97.23; 10.8.4, 5.)
- rtavasu, one who is invested in or living in harmony with *rta*.
- rtavak, true speech.
- rtajata, true birth.
- Ghrta, ghee, symbolic of the brilliance of Consciousness and milk of knowledge.
- amrta, immortal.
- rtambara, the application of *Rta* to the worshiper's life.
- ma/rtaa, mortal, human life.
- rtaya, maintaining the dynamic divine order. (RV 1.34.10; 1.121.4; 1.137.2; 1.151.3, 6; 1.153.3; 4.3.8; 4.23.10; 5.20.4; 9.17.8; 9.78.23; 10.8.4.)
- riti, style.
- anrta, that which is inconsistent with the cosmic order.
- aramkrta, purified, purification.
- arta, the absence or lack of the qualities inherent in the cosmic order
- nishkrta, accomplished or perfected in the qualities of the cosmic order.
- rtaavrdhaau, increasing *rta*.
- rtasprshia, pertaining to or touching *rta*.

Rta, and its derivations, are mentioned literally hundreds of times in the Rg Veda. The range of these derivations explain the difficulty in assigning *Rta* to a single word. In truth, *Rta* encapsulates all these concepts, and more. If forced to be reduced to a single sentence, the quotation from Pope Francis in the beginning of this chapter is the best summary of *rta*. *Rta*, the Natural Order, the Vedic dharma, encapsulates the sum total of laws which are eternal and of divine origin and fuel the internal dynamism of the Universe. The sacrificial rite is intended to reflect those laws in a ritualistic setting; and passage through the sacrifice is calculated to place the worshiper in harmony with the eternal order of things in order that those things which are true and right. *Rta* thus represents the very pith and essence of the dynamism that powers the universe.

Rta is both implemented by and fuels the divine energies of Vedic deities. For example, the laws of *Rta* lay the foundation to establish the dynamic Vedic energies inherent in Varuna, who in turn embodies the principle of *rta*. (RV 1.25.6, 8, 10; 8.27.3; 10.66.5, 8.) In implementing these established laws of *rta*, and the other incidents of *rta*, Varuna is the Lord Protector of the Vedic dharma presiding over *rta*. (RV 10.124.5.) He also:

- Gave birth to *Rta* (the Natural Order). (RV 1.105.15.)
- Establishes the paths of the planets, stars and constellations. (RV 1.24.8.)
- Establishes the Two-Dimensional Universe of Heaven and Earth. (RV 6.70.1; 7.86.1.)
- The laws regulating this dimension of the universe is implemented by Mitra-Varuna. (RV 5.13.7.)
- Establishes the Three-Dimensional Universe of the earth, mid-earth and heavens. (RV 7.87.5.)
- The laws regulating this three-dimension of the universe is also implemented by Mitra-Varuna. (RV 5.13.7; 5.62.3.)
- Provides the support of the earth. (RV 5.3.7; 7.61.4.)

A similar symbiotic relationship exists between all dynamic Vedic forces and the Vedic dharma, which is *rta*. The dynamic Vedic forces are the "seed," garbha, of *rta*. The dynamic Vedic forces which are identified as the "seed" of *rta*:

- Visnu. (RV 1.156.3.)
- Agni, the Principle of Transformation. (RV 6.48.5; 10.92.6.)
- Mitra - Varuna. (RV 6.67.4.)
- Indra and Varuna are the rulers over the newly established world, *rta*. (RV 3.30; 4.42.)

On the other hand, the dynamic Vedic forces, these seeds of *rta*, are at the same time the "first born" of *Rta* itself. Here, the Veda identifies these Vedic forces as *rta*'s first born:

- Agni, the Principle of Transformation. (RV 10.5.7.)
- The Waters. (RV 10.109.1.) In the symbolic language of the Rg Veda, "the Waters" represent, in fact, the very essence of the Vedic dharma.
- Vayu, the Principle of Vital Life Force. (RV 10.168.3.)
- Brhaspati, the Principle of Consciousness. (RV 6.73.1.)
- Prajapati. (AV 4.35.1; 12.1.6.)
- Visvakarmen. (RV 6.122.1.)
- Soma, the Principle of Divine Union and Religious Ecstasy. (RV 9.68.5.)
- The entire pantheon of dynamic Vedic forces. (RV 10.61.19.)
- A dynamic unidentified Vedic divine force called simply "the first born of *rta*." hese Vedic forces are the "first born" of *rta*. The laws of *Rta* are implemented with the assistance of primary Vedic energies:
- Indra. (RV 6.19.5.)
- Mitra-Varuna. (RV 1.15.6; 5.62.8; 8.25.2, 8.)
- Indra-Varuna. (RV 6.68.10.)
- Savitr. (RV 4.53.4.)
- Varuna, establishing the laws of *Rta* in conjunction with (Agni). (RV 1.44.14; 1.141.9.)

The Veda indeed notes the equivalence of the established laws of the dynamic cosmic order (*rta*) to the principle of Change (Agni). (RV 8.44.25.) *Rta*, the Vedic dharma, is the father of Agni, the Principle of Transformation and Change (RV 10.5.7) and Visnu. (RV 1.156.3.) Yet, although these dynamic Vedic energies implement the laws of the dynamic cosmic order, the Veda is clear that it is the Vedic dharma itself which is responsible for the birth of the Vedic forces which eventually implement its own laws. The purpose of all these Vedic energies and the dynamic cosmic order of *Rta* is to enable the worshiper to rediscover the most basic energy of the cosmos and integrate that energy into their daily lives. Modern astrophysics is just beginning to acknowledge that there had existed an unmanifest, indiscriminate mass of matter prior to the Big Bang, and that there may have been more than one Big Bang following cycles of the universe. This notion is characteristic of the Zeitgeist prior to our own, present in the Dharma and the Veda. (RV 10.129.4.)

Rta, then, is a complex, elusive, expansive, concept, implicating many deities and divine forces and encompassing the most basic features of the universe and as well as serving a basic code of conduct. This is the subject of the Asyavamasya Sukta, Sukta 164 of the First Mandala of Rg Veda. It is the subject of this book. *Rta* is the Natural Order, that Natural Order is divine, it is cosmic in its full implications. It is the Vedic dharma.

THE VEDIC DHARMA

The Asyavamasya Sukta, RV 1.164, is all about the Vedic dharma. In Vedic terms, dharma is the totality of the Natural Order. (VaS, 1.1.1.) The word itself, "dharma," however, is infrequently found in the Rg Veda. In its place, the Rg Veda spoke of *rta*, the dynamic cosmic Natural Order. References to *Rta* in the Vedas are legion. *Rta*, or derivatives of *rta*, occur well over two hundred times in the Rg Veda.

In the Vedic Dharma the anchor of the Natural Order is *Rta* itself as reflected in the Vedic deities, themselves the dynamic forces of that Natural Order which are incorporated into the lives of worshipers. The aim is that we learn from the dharma (*rta*) and live according to its highest aspirations. It was assumed that human beings are not only composed of the same ingredients of the universe but is also ruled by the same universal principles. The principal subject of the Asyavamasya Sukta is to discover the darkest, deepest principles of the cosmos, of the Vedic dharma. The purpose of this search is to discover the relation of the cosmos to the Natural Order (*rta*) and relate that Natural Order to the material world and to the people who inhabit it who incorporate those precepts into their lives. Dharma is that enlightenment and understanding obtained from the Natural Order (*rta*). (VaS, 1.1.2.)

The mantra ("rc") which follows begins our exploration into the components of this Natural Order. If the Natural Order can be viewed as an automobile, this rc (mantra) discusses the ingredients and additives of the fuel for that vehicle. The journey begins.

The Asyavamasya Sukta

(After the translation by Ralph Griffith)

This is the Asyavamasya Sukta, which provides the outlines for the Vedic dharma, the Natural Order (*rta*). All further references are from the Rig Veda ("RV"):

RV 1.164.1:

Surya (Energy) has two brothers: Agni (the Principle of Change) and the other brother which carries ghee. In these I saw the Lord having Seven Sons.

RV 1.164.2:

A horse having seven names carries a yoke having three wheels.
The wheels never get old and never decays.

RV 1.164.3:

The seven horses carry the seven sisters who have the "seven utterances."

RV 1.164.4:

Who has seen the first-born having bones born from that being having no bones?

I ask the Rishiis because I do not know.

RV 1.164.5:

My mind cannot conceive the principles which pervade and rule over the Creation.

RV 1.164.6:

Not seeing I ask the Rishiis who see and have seen.
What holds the Creation together?

What is the One (ekam), which is the unborn?

RV 1.164.7:

Let him who knows declare the dynamics of Energy (Surya) and explain how water can be evaporated by the rays of the Sun.

RV 1.164.8:

The mother (earth) worships the father (Sun) that she may receive water.
The earth receives this water by "impregnation."
He anticipates her needs with his mind and communicates one to the other.

RV 1.164.9:

The mother (Earth) is yoked on the right side of the axle.
Its womb is rested in the clouds.
The calf (rain) bellows in three places.
It looks to its mother which manifests in three spaces.

RV 1.164.10:

The One living in the skies has three mothers and three fathers.
These parents speak in a voice that comprehends all but does not move.

RV 1.164.11:

Formed with twelve spokes, by length of time, unweakened, this wheel of order (*rta*) rolls around heaven.
Agni stands joined in pairs together, seven hundred and twenty sons.

RV 1.164.12:

The father has five feet and twelve forms in the farthest end of the hemisphere.
The father consists of water.
He is placed on a chariot having seven wheels.

RV 1.164.13

All beings reside in a five-spoked revolving wheel that is not heated.

RV 1.164.14:

The wheel rolls on.
The Ten yoke the wheel upwards.

RV 1.164.15

Of the seven, six are twins and the seventh is born alone and apart from the others.
The six are placed in their proper position and move, changing form.

RV 1.164.16

Those [asterisms] that have become females, become male.
The ignorant do not understand this, but those who can see, the learned, do.

RV 1.164.17:

The cow stands up carrying its calf.
Where is it going?
It is going to the herd.

RV 1.164.18:

There are twelve fellies and a single wheel, and there are three naves.
Who can understand this?
Therein are three hundred and sixty spokes which cannot be loosened.

RV 1.164.19:

That which descends will ascend, and that which ascends will descend.
Conjunction and unity (Indra) in conjunction with Divine Ecstacy (Soma) create the regions.
They carry the rays of light to travel in the far reaches of the space like yoked horses.

RV 1.164.20:

There are two birds sitting on a tree.
One is eating, and the other one is not eating but merely looks around.

RV 1.164.21:

There where the birds sing the Lord Protector of all enters me, ignorant though I am, and I attain wisdom.

RV 1.164.22:

On that tree the birds rest, inspiring each other.
On the top of the tree are berries.
If one does not reach the top of the tree, one does not reach the Father.

RV 1.164.23:

Those who understand that how Gayatri, Tristup or Jagati are based attain immortal life.

RV 1.164.24:

At the sacrifice the prayers are constructed in a Gayatri metre.
The saman chant is constructed in the Tristup metre.
The verses are in Anubaak metre.
One syllable consists of seven metres.

RV 1.164.25:

The flowing water is established in heaven by the Jagati metre.
The Sun rests everywhere in Rathantar.
There are three parts to Gayatri.
It is the superior metre.

RV 1.164.26:

I call the cow that is easily milked, that I may use one good hand to milk her.
May Savitr produce superior milk for us.

RV 1.164.27:

The cow desires her calf. May the cow give her milk to the Asvins.

RV 1.164.28:

The cow calls out for her calf.
She licks her calf on the forehead, utters a cry and gives it milk.

RV 1.164.29:

The calf bellows as well.
The cow is attached to the calf and cries softly and mindfully, shining radiantly.

RV 1.164.30:

Life, imbued with breath, moves firm and fast, and rests in the middle.
The Immortal Self, which wanders about at its own volition, and mortal beings both arise from the same source.

RV 1.164.31:

I beheld Surya, the untiring Protector, traveling upwards and downwards in his path.
Emitting rays that reach everywhere, they reach the middle.

RV 1.164.32:

He who has made this state of things, does not know it.
It is hidden from him who see this state of things.
He who is covered in his mother's womb has many offspring and is born to suffering and evil.

RV 1.164.33:

The sky is my father; the earth is my mother.
Between them, in the middle, the earth and the sky, held upside down, and is the source (yoni) of my birth.
The father impregnates the daughter.

RV 1.164.34:

I seek the farthest limits of earth.
I wonder where is the inner essence (nahbih) of world.
I seek the seamen of a strong horse.
I seek the Word, Logos, the guiding First Principle which powers the world.

RV 1.164.35:

The altar is the farthest limit of the earth.
The sacrifice is the inner essence of the world.
Soma is the seamen of the strong horse.

RV 1.164.36:

Seven half-seeds, the inner essence of the world, perform their functions according to the command of Vishnu.
With their thoughts, they pervade and encompass all the universe.

RV 1.164.37:

I did not understand this all and roamed aimlessly in hiding attempting to understand this.
Then the first born of *Rta* consisting of its laws came to me and I began to understand the Word and participate in the speech.

RV 1.164.38:

With up and down movements I become immortal through svadha, even though I remain a mortal person.
These up and down movements are eternal movements and go in different directions.
They understand, yet do not understand, each other.

RV 1.164.39:

The gods sit and take their supreme position on hearing the rcs of the Veda.
What can a person do if they do not know this?
Those that do understand the rcs sit with the gods.

RV 1.164.40:

May you be happy eating the barley grass.
The cow will not be harmed and allowed to eat the grass, drink the water and wander about.

RV 1.164.41:

The ruddy cow utters the luminous word and makes a sound.
This word speaks in a one-footed, two-footed, four-footed, eight-footed, and nine-footed phrase, in thousands of letters.

RV 1.164.42:

The ocean flows from this ruddy cow and flows in the four directions.
The whole of existence flows from that ocean.

RV 1.164.43:

I see the smoke rising from the cow-dung.
The heroes have cooked the spotted bull.
They become the first dharmas.

RV 1.163.44:

The three look down on the seasons of the earth.

One shears the ground; another gazes upon the entire universe.
The other's motion is seen but form is not.

RV 1.164.45:

Speech is divided into four parts.
Three of those parts are occult and subtle.
The last part is uttered by people.

RV 1.164.46:

They speak of Indra, Mitra, Varuna (Lord Protector of the Dynamic Cosmic Order), and fire (Agni). The learned speak of many names, but there is only one.
The one is a winged bird.

RV 1.164.47:

The ruddy birds raise to heaven on the dark path, clothed in the waters.
The birds return from the realm of the divine cosmic order.
When they arrive, the surface of the world is blanketed with ghee.

RV 1.164.48:

Twelve spokes, one wheel, three axles, who really understand this?
There, three hundred and sixty are placed, firm and steady.

RV 1.164.49:

Saraswati is the beast, eternal, receives riches,
and is the giver of nourishment to the entire superior.

RV 1.164.50:

The gods perform sacrifice with sacrifice.
They are the first dharma.

RV 1.164.51:

This water goes up and down daily.
The Parjanyas enliven the earth;
The fire enlivens the heaven.

RV 1.164.52:

The divine bird, the child of the waters, brings satisfaction
in the rainy season.
I invoke Saraswati again and again.

The Vedic Dharma

RV 1.164.1:

Surya (Energy) has two brothers:
Agni (the Principle of Change) and the other brother which carries ghee.
In these I saw the Lord having Seven Sons.

A MODEST INTERPRETATION:

RV 1.164.1 discusses the three subtle processes that run the cosmic universe. The rc (mantra) states the Natural Order (*rta*) is a product of the processes from three deities:

- Surya.
- Agni.
- Ghrta.

First, an explanation of the Vedic deities. The deities in the Vedic pantheon are usually portrayed as mythological beings. At best this is an incomplete treatment of their import, at worst a misconception. The Vedic deities are active forces, powers, and processes which are constantly at work maintaining the continued operation of the Natural Order, which is sometimes called the Vedic dharma, which is conceptionally called "*rta*." These Vedic deities take the form of active Principles, subtle principles which provide the substructure of the universe and are represented by the various Vedic deities. From this substructure the Vedic deities sometimes physically manifest as natural phenomena, always originate from the subtle principles from which these physical phenomena arise, but other times remain as subtle, intangible principles only. There are many active principles, of course, and some of these Principles are actual, tangible forces of nature, such as

- Mass.
- Number.
- Universe.

Some of these forces appear as categories of natural phenomena, such as

- Precipitation.
- Geo-Thermal Activity.
- Seismic Activity.
- Wind.
- Fire, and the rest of the elements, and the like.

Some forces represent categories of purely intangible, subtle, concepts, such as

- Word
- Thought
- Action.
- Beauty.
- Discrimination or understanding.
- Truth.
- Bliss.
- Regeneration.

… and most importantly …

- Word (as Logos or Vac, or, the Vedic dharma).

Some are mixed principles encompassing both tangible and intangible elements:

- Time.
- Space.

- Energy.
- Light.

Think of the Vedic deities such as Agni, Indra, and the others as the repositories of these active forces and principles. Indeed, they are active forces of the principles these forces represent and are constantly at work to empower the Natural Order (*rta*). Through the energies of these active Vedic principles, the Vedic deities keep the machine of the universe running, functional, and operational. Surya and Agni are just two of those forces which drive the Vedic dharma, the Natural Order (*rta*). Other Vedic deities serve in a similar manner. The most prominent are

- Indra whose powers include two differing but related forces. One, he is the dynamic force of Conjunction and Unity, the characteristics of which are subsumed in Vitality (Bala). Two, he is the dynamic force of the Articulation of Mind and Matter. These elements are subsumed in the Principle of Increase. They are only the most prominent forces and principles Indra represents. Indra is a very complex and multifaceted Vedic force.
- Soma is the dynamic force of Ecstasy, Purification and Divine Union.

Rta as the Natural Order is present in the entire array of the divine Vedic forces. Each and every Vedic force has meaning and represents a separate natural principle that contributes to the continued operation of that order and the universe of which it services. You will be encountering other Vedic forces in this exploration. For now, the only deities (Principles) we are concerned with here are Surya and Agni.

RV 1.164.1 deals with three Vedic forces which serve as the internal combustion, the very fabric, of the Natural Order, dharma (*rta*):

- Surya, a deity, is the Vedic force and principle which embodies Energy.
- Agni, a complex deity, is the first brother in this rc, and is the Vedic force which embodies the principle of Change or Flux.
- Ghrta.

Surya

Surya is the Vedic force, which represents the energy emanating from the Sun. Surya is called the "invoker." The invoker is called the highest deity according to Sayana, the Medieval commentator. Surya is also known as Aditya, Bhanu or Ravi Visvasvan, is the chief solar deity in Hinduism, and generally refers to the Sun. The Rishiis recognized the Sun is the source of life on earth. It's one thing to call Surya the "invoker," but what does that term mean? In keeping with its capacity as an astronomical body, Surya (Energy) has the following qualities as the "invoker":

- Surya measures the days. (RV 1.50.7.) Surya, the Sun, assures the progression of day after night, night before the day. There is something more going on with this progression of day and night. The seemingly unending progression of day and night has great spiritual power to transform the worshiper and is a formidable implement in the worshiper's path to salvation. This has as much to do with the intense meditative practice described in another terrestrial fire, Usasanakta. According to that practice, the worshiper meditates on the constant regularity of the passage of days, nights, weeks, etc., and as a result of this intense meditation concludes there is no difference between the future and the past. In arriving at this conclusion the worshiper pierces through time to eternity and dwells in the eternal present. *(see,* Weil, *Imitations of Christianity,* p. 94.)
- Prolongs the days of life. (RV 8.48.7.) Surya, the Sun, with his sunlight, supplies the requisites to energize the life of the worshiper.
- Drives away sickness, disease and other evils. (RV 10.37.4.) With the energies supplied to Surya all sicknesses and diseases are driven away.
- Is the Visvakarmen, the Creator of all. (RV 10.170.4.) Surya, the Sun, is the Creator of the material world. The Rishiis understood the difference between the subtle and material creators of existence. They assigned several Vedic forces as creators and suppliers of the subtle foundation of the Vedic dharma. The Rishiis additionally understood that without the Sun, Surya, all life would cease on earth.

- The source of all actions. (RV 10.170.4.)
- Establishes movement in all things. (RV 1.50.10; 1.115.1; 10.37.10.) As part of the material basis of the Vedic dharma, Surya, the Sun, provides the impetus for movements in the material world. This movement owes much as because of Surya's role as Creator of the material world as to the progression of days and nights. Creation becomes the first principle of all that follows, movement being one.
- Surya is described as the "soul of all that moves," which is to say that it provides the inner catalyst that creates all movement, from the tiniest atom to the largest astrological body. (RV 1.115.1.)

There is an intimate relationship between the Invoker (Surya) and the first brother (Agni):

- Surya is the light of the Sun which is converted into the heat of Agni. (RV 10.114.1.) The Vedic force of Agni operates on several levels. The Vedic force of Agni is present in all three levels of existence in the Vedic dharma — Heaven, the Mid-World, and Earth. On a terrestrial level the Vedic force of Agni (heat or physical fire) appears as a result of the Vedic force of Surya, the Sun.
- Agni is the heat of the Sun. (SPB 2.3.1.30.) In the multifaceted character of the Vedic force of Agni, the Celestial manifestation of Agni supplies the subtle foundation for the heat emitted from the Sun.

Agni, the Principle of Change and Transformation

Thus, we segue into Agni, the first "brother." The first of Surya's "brothers," Agni has the quality of lightning:

- Agni, commonly related to fire, is associated with lightning. (SPB 10.6.2.11.)
- In a passage pregnant with individual meaning, the fire of Agni is kindled by the breath, the wind by the fire, the Sun by the winds, the moon by the sun, the stars by the moon, and the lightning by the Stars. (SPB 10.6.2.11.) In other words, Agni is powered by the elements of the natural (*rta*).

37

The main active principle for Agni is Change and Transformation. Agni is associated with this material world. In his dominion over this world, Agni exercises his dominion as the Principle of Change, encompassing the constant change and flux of the sensible world, and informs the mental and spiritual transformation of the mind and soul of the worshiper. Lightning is an incidental characteristic for Agni. This aspect of the Principle of Change is inherent in Agni Vasivanara. (SPB 10.6.4.1.) Agni's predominance in the Vedas is the acknowledgment that change is the pervasive principle in the universe.

In Sanskrit "Agne" means "fire." Agni is traditionally mentioned as the god of fire. Classical grammarians, however, derive Agni's name from the root, "ang." (Sastry, Collected Works, Vol. IV, (1983).) From the root ang the word Angara for "charcoal" is derived. The charcoal is the remnants of the Sacrificial or any Fire, which is representative of Knowledge and Self-Sacrifice. Just as fire consumes wood, leaving its essential elements in the form of charcoal and ash, that same process is in operation and reduces the form and substance of the universe to its essential elements. Embers are the heated coals once the fire has subsided, and after the embers have subsided, charcoal remains after the Sacrificial Fire has been ignited. If the Sacrificial Fire represents knowledge, charcoal represents the final irreducible essence of that knowledge.

Fire is the principal medium for change. As a physical phenomenon, fire is constantly changing shape and form, and it is one of the few agents which can change another substance and reduce it to its most elemental physical substances, instantaneously and seemingly at will. Agni is Fire, which is why Agni is the principle of Change and transformation.

What follows are the attributes of the principle of Change as embodied in Agni. From the simple root of "ang," the various aspects of Agni are derived:

- Anga, signifying brilliance or effulgence, specifically to describe the aspect of Change in the light of consciousness. (RV 1.1.6; 1.84.7, 8, 19; 1.118.3;1.164.7; 2.41.10; 3.33.11; 3.48.5; 5.3.11; 6.44.10;6.50.10; 6.52.3; 6.72.5; 7.20.9; 7.56.2; 7.91.1; 8.6.26;8.7.2; 8.80.5; 8.96.13; 10.4.4; 10.42.3; 10.54.4; 10.64.13; 10.79.4; 10.129.7; 10.131.2; 10.149.3.)
- Angdh, the attribute of resplendence, again, expressed in association of consciousness. (RV 9.5.10.)

- Angdhve, signifying the flash of revelation. (RV 10.100.10.)
- The Angiras, the family of Vedic Rishis. (RV 1.1.6; 1.74.5; 2.23.8; 4.9.7; 5.11.1; 6.2.10; 8.60.2; 8.74.11; 8.75.5; 8.102.17.)
- Angirastama, the mystic essence of the Agniras Rishis. (RV 1.75.2; 8.43.18;8.43.27.)
- Angiraso, that aspect of Angiras in possession of super-human intellectual power obtained through intense yoga and meditation. (RV 1.62.2; 1.71.2; 3.53.7; 4.2.15;4.3.11; 5.11.6; 6.65.5;7.42.1; 10.14.6; 10.67.2; 10.78.6; 10.108.9.)
- Angiro, the divine reflection of Angiras imbued with the glory of Change. (RV 1.31.11; 1.112.18; 4.3.15; 5.2.8; 5.21.1; 6.16.11.)

The simple association of Agni, however, to fire is superficial and merely scratches the surface of its full meaning. There are five attributes to the Principle of Change which permeate the dynamic force inherent in Agni:

- One, Agni represents the internal, gastric, digestive fire, generally referred to in the Rg Veda as agnir or agnim.
- Two, Agni represents the cosmic life force in all its permutations which is inherent in the universe, signified in the Rg Veda as agnih.
- Three, Agni represents the force of the light of consciousness, signified in the Rg Veda as agnim.
- Four, Agni represents the sacrificial fire, signified in the Rg Veda as agnim.
- Five, Agni represents physical fire.

These five attributes are the basis components of the Principle of Change. A vastly overlooked Nineteenth Century Vedic scholar, Pandit Vidyavacaspati Madhusdan Ojha, assigns mrtyu, change or impermanence, as the defining characteristic of Change (Agni). The pervasion of the active principle inherent in Agni runs across every level of existence:

On a material, microcosmic level Change represents the digestive fire which supports the individual and operates the material world.

- In a mental level Change represents the light of knowledge.
- On a spiritual level, Change (Agni) represents the fire which burns away impurities, sins, of the worshiper, providing the forgiveness of sins.
- On cosmic level Change (Agni) represents the Cosmic Fire.
- On a transcendent level, Agni represents the burning of the seeds of past karma from previous lives.

These attributes proceed in a linear fashion. Agni is identified with Fire. Because fire is the ultimate transformative agent, Agni takes many forms:

- Common Fire is the symbol for Change. Physical fire completely consumes whatever meets its path. The flames transform their objects into ashes and smoke to where it is reduced to its most basic elements.
- Physical, common, fire, contains the dynamic which is translated to the gastric, digestive fire, which transform food into energy.
- The energy is characteristic of the effulgence of light, representative of the speed and impulse of light of consciousness, namely the speed with which the synapses in the human brain spark.
- The light of consciousness is symbolized in the sacrificial fire, which is also symbolic of the cosmic life force which sustains the universe and all creatures therein.
- In a sacrificial context, while the sacrificial fire is representative of other aspects, the sacrificial fire is at essence symbolic of the purification of the worshiper, his soul and body. The fire purifies and extinguishes the sins of the worshiper. The flames themselves are brilliant, glowing and constantly changing form.

The following then are the qualities which exist in Agni:

- The gastric fire is symbolic of the energy released by the power of fire.
- The strength of the conflagration is representative of the awesome power fire can exhibit.

- The brilliance of the flames matches the association of light to consciousness, used so many times, not only in the Vedas, but in Vedic thought in general.
- The sacrificial fire is the icon of purification and redemption.

Paradoxically, the impermanent nature of change creates its own permanence. This permanence is evoked by the introduction of polarity. In the process of change, the polarized qualities are transformed into their opposites. This process of reversal is one of the essential processes present in the Vedic dharma. The process of reversal the Principle of Change becomes an eternal, unchangeable, never-changing process.

The metaphysical meaning of Agni is sometimes articulated in terms of food. In the Brhadaranyakaupanishad, the eater of food is that which produces food again and again. (BU 1.5.2.) In his Commentary to the Brhadaranyakaupanishad, Sankara, the great Vedic thinker of Advaita Nondualism, regards Food as the object of the enjoyment of food. Sankara was not just trying to be obtuse. The food and object of food distinction is emblematic of a deeper process found in the Vedic dharma. ((BU 1.5.2.) This simile demonstrates the distinction of the Subject (the Eater of Food) and the object (Food). This is how Food is considered in the Vedas.

A principle function of Agni arises from this understanding of food. Agni is the eater of food which transforms the food eaten (digestive, gastric fire) into the vital life force, the energy of which is transformed into the force of the light of consciousness. This process, in turn, transforms simple, physical fire, into the sacrificial fire, which represents this entire process of Change. The scope of the Eternal Law of Change thus encompasses the body, mind, and spirit.

Saunaka, a Mediaeval author, lists the Vedic divinities and forces over which Agni holds. dominion and whose operative principle prevails. Agni, the Principle of Change, presides over these divine forces based on his many manifestations. There are three principal manifestations of Change (Agni): the celestial, the "Middle" Agni, and the terrestrial Agni. (BD, 1.91.) Each manifestation contains its own special quality. Suci Agni, the celestial, heavenly aspect of Change (Agni), presides over these divinities: (BD, 1.19.91, et seq.)

- Bharati, the divinities "Knowing the minds of gods;" Omniscient; all-knowing. (RV 1.64.13; 1.96.3; 1.1043; 1.109.7; 1.112.21; 1.136.1; 1.152.3; 2.14.2, 8; 224.2; 2.26.3; 2.37.1; 3.10.5; 3.33.11, 12; 3.52.8, 24; 4.17.9; 5.11.1; 5.32.9; 5.43.3; 5.54.14; 6.16.4; 7.8.4; 7.24.2; 7.33.6; 7.46.1; 8.100.3; 9.48.3, 4; 9.97.1; 9.106.3; 10.40.6, 8; 10.75.1; 10.76.4; 10.100.2; 10.138.6; 10.147.4.)
- Agni Vanaspati, the "Middle Agni," resides in the firmament presides over these divinities with the following qualities:
- Sarasvati, the Power of Consciousness to Hear the Truth. (RV 1.13.9.)
- Tvstr, the Architect, "Fashioner of Forms," (BD 1.84) of the Universe.
- Tvastr, the Creator of the Universe, the Demiurge. (RV 1.13.10; 1.20.6; 1.22.9; 1.32.2; 1.52.7; 1.61.6; 1.80.14; 1.84.15; 1.85.9; 1.95.2, 5; 1.114.10; 1.161.4, 5; 1.162.3, 19; 1.186.6; 1.188.9; 2.1.5; 2.3.9; 2.23.17; 2.31.4; 2.36.3; 3.48.9; 3.54.12; 3.55.19; 4.18.9; 4.33.5, 6; 4.42.3; 5.31.4; 5.41.8; 5.46.4; 6.17.10; 6.47.19; 6.50.13; 6.52.11; 7.34.20, 21, 22; 7.35.6; 8.26.21, 22; 8.102.8; 9.5.9; 9.81.4; 10.2.7; 10.10.5; 10.17.1; 10.18.6; 10.46.9; 10.48.3; 10.49.5; 10.53.9; 10.64.10; 10.65.10; 10.66.3; 10.92.11; 10.110.9; 10.125.2; 10.184.1.)

The terrestrial, material manifestation of Change (Agni) presides over the following divinities possessing the following qualities:

- Apva, "Filled," "Fullness," "Plenum," having the quality of Pervasiveness. (RV 1.52.13; 1.115.1; 4.14.2; 4.4.5.3; 9.97.5.)
- Atithi, symbolizing the "Guest" of human dwellings, constant presence. (RV 5.1.8; 6.2.7; 7.8.4; 7.9.3.)
- Barhi, representing the inner seat (of grass) wherein the vision of Agni is made. (RV 1.13.5,7; 145.9; 1.63.7; 1.83.6; 1.85.6; 1.108.4; 1.116.1; 1.135.1; 1.142.5; 1.144.6; 1.177.4; 1.188.4; 2.3.8; 2.36.2; 2.41.13; 2.34.8, 11; 3.9.9; 3.13.1; 3.14; 1; 3.41.2, 9; 3.53.1; 4.9.1; 5.26.8; 5.44.3; 5.46.5; 6.11.5; 6.23.7; 6.52.7; 6.67.2; 7.2.3, 8, 11; 7.11.2; 7.17.1; 7.39.2; 7.43.2; 7.57.2; 7.91.4; 8.1.8; 8.27.1, 6; 8.28.1;

8.31.6; 8.45.1; 8.60.1; 8.65.2; 8.93.25; 9.87.4; 10.30.15; 10.52.6; 10.70.8, 11; 10.110.8; 10.188.1.)

- Dhumaketu, "Special Vibratory" (dhuma) + "knowledge" (ketu), the vibration of Knowledge envisions Change (Agni) as the "smoke bearer." (RV 1.27.11; 10.4.5; 10.12.2.) Smoke indicative, as a later chapter explains, the presence of consciousness.

- Grhapati, Change (Agni) as the Sacrificial Fire. (RV 1.12.6; 1.36.5; 1.60.4; 2.1.2; 4.9.4; 4.11.5; 5.8.1, 2; 6.15.13, 42; 6.48.8; 6.53.2; 7.1.1; 7.15.2; 7.16.5; 8.102.1; 10.118.6; 10.122.1.)

- Idhma, Change (Agni) representing Fuel of Fire. (RV 4.2.6; 4.12.2; 6.20.13; 8.42.2; 10.90.6.)

- Ila, an epithet of Change (Agni) representing the Power of Consciousness to envision the truth. (RV 1.13.9;1.31.11; 1.40.4; 1.149.9; 2.1.11; 2.3.8; 3.4.8; 3.7.5; 4.50.8; 5.5.8; 5.41.8; 7.2.8; 7.16.8; 8.31.4; 10.36.5; 10.110.8.)

- Jatavedas, a prevalent epithet, signifying the "Knower of all things born." (RV 6.4.2; 6.10.1; 6.12.4; 6.15.13; 7.9.4; 7.12.2 1.77.5; 2.4.1; 3.1.20; 4.1.20; 4.58.8; ; 10.45.1; 10.61.14; 10.83.2; 10.88.4.) Jatadevas also means, "The light of consciousness." (RV 3.17.4.)

- Kavi, another name for the Rishis.

- Pracetas, that aspect of Change (Agni) implicating omniscience. (RV 1.24.14; 1.120.1; 10.7.5; 10.117.6.)

- Svadha (RV 1.6.4; 1.33.11; 1.88.6; 1.165.5, 9; 2.35.7; 3.51.11; 4.33.6; 4.52.6; 5.34.1; 6.2.8; 7.8.3; 7.56.13; 8.20.7; 8.32.6, 19; 8.88.5; 9.103.5; 9.113.10; 10.129.5; 10.157.5), defined as a power which upholds its nature, following its own law or nature, svadha refers to the essential nature of dynamic Vedic forces in the Vedic pantheon including Agni. On a personal level, svadha refers to the incorporation and implementation of the spiritual qualities present in the Vedic divine forces into the life of the worshiper.

- Svahakritis, the maker of offerings, from "Offering" (svaha) + "maker" (kriti). (RV 1.188.11.)

- Tanunapi, that aspect of Change (Agni) meaning "The summer Sun" or "Son of the Body of the aspirant." (RV 1.13.2; 1.142.2.)

- Tvasta. (RV 3.4.9; 5.5.9; 7.2.9; 10.70.9.)

- Usasanakta is "Dawn and Night." ((RV 1.122.2; 2.3.6; 4.55.3; 5.41.7; 7.2.6; 10.36.1; 10.70.6; 10.110.6.) Night and Dawn are "firmly established" in the material aspect of Agni (BD, 3.2.7), meaning that the process of Change and all the internal processes in Agni provide the repeated occurrences of the night preceding the dawn (BD, 3.2.9, 10), much like a revolving door. Hence, the appellation of dawn and night as the "divine doors." (BD, 3.2.6.)
- Vaisvanara, a principal aspect of Change (Agni). (RV 1.59.3, 4, 6, 7; 1.98.1, 2; 3.2.1, 11, 12; 3.3.1, 5, 11; 3.26.1, 2, 3; 4.5.1, 2; 5.15.13; 6.7.1, 2, 6, 7; 6.8.1, 2, 3, 4; 6.9.1, 7; 7.5.1, 2, 5; 7.6.6, 7; 7.13.1; 7.49.4; 8.30.4; 9.61.16; 10.45.12; 10.88.12, 13, 14.) Vaisvanara is defined as the Terrestrial Fire produced from the Aerial Fire, the Fire of the Firmament, and Celestial Fire. (BD, 2.18; Nir. 7.6; T.S., 2.2.5.) Vaisvanara is elsewhere defined as the digestive fire.
- Vanaspati, defined as the "Lord of Beauty." (RV 10.172.1.)

The Principle of Change (Agni) in his main manifestations therefore implicates many aspects and characteristics. These aspects are applied to the material world. In the terrestrial aspect of the principle of change Agni is applied to a material world as mass and matter. This is tantamount to saying that the material world is subject to constant change and flux. It is the principle by which all material objects are subject to, the endless cycles of change, generation and degradation.

The manifestation of Agni as the Principle of Change is created three ways:

- By self-creation, by Agni, when Agni (Fire) is ignited. (RV1.12.6.)
- Spontaneously, when the rubbing sticks, the aranis, are kindled. This has been called, as referenced in this rc, lightning. (SPB 6.1.3.14.)
- Spontaneously, when nourished in the sacrificial fire, with ghee. Thus, enters the second brother.

Ghee, Ghrta, the symbol of the Light of Consciousness

Thus, enter the third element. The third element is the second brother who carries "ghee on its back," an especially opaque phrase. Ghrta or ghee is not a deity. It is a subtle attribute incorporating the quality of Effulgence or Illumination and is present in the other Vedic deities and to all sentient and insentient being in the Natural Order. Linguistically, Ghrta it is a derivative from *rta*, the Natural Order. Ghrta is made up of two roots, "gh" + rta. "Gh," is the root meaning, "to go," "to hasten towards," and "to sprinkle." *Rta* is the cosmic order, the Natural Order. Ghrta, ghee, then, is symbolic of "that which hastens towards or go to *rta*" "that which sprinkles upon the cosmic order." Ghrta literally is that substance which showers the world order with illumination and brilliance.

There are four aspects of ghrta discussed in RV 4.58.1:

- Ghrta is the highest form of offering to the divine.
- Ghrta is that which is recovered by Indra after battling Vala.
- Ghrta refers to the cows recovered from the Panis, released by Indra typically with Vajra (RV 1.11.5; 2.24.6; 8.3.4; 1.93.4; 4.58.4), and the waters released when Indra slew Vrtra. (RV 5.29.3; 1.52.8; 1.61.10; 1.32.2 (releasing the waters to the ocean); 1.32.12 (the seven rivers); 2.12.12 (same); 1.61.10; 3.31.1 (releasing the Vipas and Sutudri Rivers); 3.34.9; 3.31.21; 3.34.4; 3.44.5; 4.16.8; 3.54.15; 2.19.2; 8.63.3.)
- Ghrta is the inspired speech from the Rishis.

Ghrta is above all emblematic of light. There are two aspects to Ghrta.

- Ghrta is an amalgam of the adamantine powers and qualities symbolic of the effulgence and brilliance of the primal Light of Knowledge, while the first brother, Agni, the principle of change and flux, is effulgence and brilliance itself.
- Ghrta is the very embodiment of rebirth and renewal, symbolized ritualistically when the initiate is smeared with butter or ghee. (AB, 1.1.3.)

The two brothers, Agni and Ghrta, are bound together by Surya, the purveyor of effulgence and brilliance. Like a nuclear reaction, the combined power of these two brothers is pure energy. These elements interacting together form the foundation of the Vedic dharma. Surya, the inherent principle of the energy packed in the Sun, empowers the other two brothers who thereupon nourishes every object in Creation.

There is a modern correlate. According to modern physics there is an equivalence between space and pure energy, reflected in Einstein's interpretation of the Riemann Curve. (Rovelli, *Seven Brief Lessons on Physics* (2015), p. 7.) RV 1.164.1 presents the Vedic version of this theory. Here, RV 1.164.1 says that Energy (Surya) is a function of the Principle of Change (Terrestrial Agni, i.e., Mass) and the lustrous brilliance of the primal light of knowledge (Ghrta). RV 1.164.1 predates the advent of relativity by millennia.

Relativity sought to explain the fabric of space-time as a function of the most powerful forces of the universe. These forces are part and parcel of the Vedic dharma (*rta*). An understanding and channeling of the principles in this rc (mantra) produces immortality, which in the coded language of the Veda means liberation and salvation. Einstein sought to explain gravity as the basis of matter but failed to explain the forces behind the gravitational pull of bodies. The Asyavamasya Sukta fills this gap by demonstrating that the basis of the Vedic dharma which is the basis for the material universe is the energy reflected in the elements described in this rc. According to the Veda, the worshiper receives spiritual benefits from the light Agni receives from Savitr. Once it is received by Agni, as the agent for transformation and change, that light becomes the equivalent to gold. (RV 1.46.10.) "Gold" is a metaphor for liberation and salvation. Through the light of gold, the worshiper arrives at heaven (TB 3.8.22.3; 3.12.5.10; SPB 13.2.2.16), which in the coded language of the Vedas meaning that the worshiper is liberated or receives salvation.

Another clue to the true significance to this rc (mantra) can be obtained from the *Xiuzhen houbian*, an esoteric commentary on the Dao, the functional equivalent of dharma (*rta*), written circa 1798. In the *Xiuzhen houbian*, the distinction was made between *xiantian*, the pre-celestial domain, and *houtian*, the post celestial domain. *Xiantian* is that region before the generation of the cosmos where the Dao does not exist, only non-being, the principle to which it pertains. (Pregadio, trans., *Cultivating the Tao* (2013), p. 3.) This unmanifested state is remarkably like that stage in the evolution of the cosmos in the Vedic tradition where being nor non-being existed. (RV 10.129.1.) Once creation is generated, *houtian*, the post celestial domain, and the Dao, appears. There are three constituent forces present in *xiantian* responsible for the appearance of *houbian*, the manifest world. Similarly, the three active forces in this rc (mantra) are responsible for the creation of the Vedic manifest world.

The rc (mantra) ends with the worshiper seeing "the Lord having Seven Sons." This is a reference to the Seven-Dimension universe, another cardinal number of the Vedic dharma, which is coded language for transcendent existence. Since the Lord in this instance means Surya, the Sun, perhaps the "seven sons" is a reference to the members of the planetary system. Nevertheless, there is an entire body of knowledge concerning the number seven. This is the topic of RV 1.164.3.

The rc (mantra) therefore provides the first fundamental components of dharma, the Natural Order (*rta*). Articulated in the language of modern physics, *rta*, Natural Order, consists of

- Mass, symbolized by Agni, the Vedic principle of Change;
- Pure Energy, symbolized by Surya; and
- Ghrta, the light of consciousness.

This rc (mantra) is thus an introduction into the Natural Order and describes its three main components therein: Surya, Energy; Agni, Mass; and Grhta, the light of consciousness.

The next rc (mantra) describes another fundamental truth of the Vedic Natural Order — that there is not one but a multiplicity of alternate universes.

RV 1.164.2:

A horse having seven names carries a yoke having three wheels.
The wheels never get old and never decays.

White Tiger is at the Pleiades, its number is seven.
It is autumn, the awns, Dui, West, and *you*.

Cantong qi, The Seal of the Unity of Three, 3.79:5 -6, Pregadio, trans.

A MODEST INTERPRETATION:

Vedic Multi-Universes

This rc (mantra) introduces us to two dimensions of the Vedic dharma — the Three- Dimensional Universe and the Seven Dimensional Universe. The contours of these dimensions well be shaped throughout this volume.

When Hamlet said, "There are more things in heaven and earth, Horacio, than are dreamt of in your philosophy," it was meant as a criticism to Horacio's difficulty in explaining in a logically coherent way the apparition of Hamlet's father which had just appeared. Hamlet posits other worlds, unseen but present, nonetheless. The thought that there is more to everyday life can be applied in many contexts in the Vedic world-view. Perhaps the most daring is the multi-universes present in the Natural Order (*rta*).

Much as in modern Quantum Mechanics theory, dharma, the divine dynamic cosmic order (*rta*), leaves open the existence of many possible, parallel universes. The Vedas do not contemplate a single universe. The

Vedic Natural Order (*rta*) consists of a series of parallel multi-universes. The Vedic dharma is like an onion. As in an onion, when you peel one layer off, another one appears, and below that, another, and another, until the very core of the onion is reached. In the Vedic dharma, these multi-universes consist of various levels of subtlety. They start with the physical world we all wake up to every morning, and progress thereafter to deeper and deeper levels, each level increasing in subtlety, until reaching a level beyond all time and space, a level of Pure Being.

This cosmological scheme coincides with the worshiper's quest for spiritual liberation. As applied to the worshiper, these multiple layers of reality begin with the very substratum of the phenomenal, material world (the Two-Dimensional Universe). This substratum is fused into the shapes and forms of that material world (the Three-Dimensional Universe), is informed by the subtle, metaphysical basis of the material world (the Five-Dimensional Universe), and then leaps beyond the material confines of material space and time to the transcendent world (the Seven-Dimensional Universe). Much like the ascent of a spiritual ladder of John Climacus, the quest for spiritual fulfillment is a journey upwards where the soul is progressively refined and purified until finally liberated from the endless cycles of rebirths found in the material world. As the worshiper's soul is further purified so does it progress to a higher dimension of dharma, the Natural Order (*rta*).

Therefore, spiritual liberation according to the Vedic dharma, the Natural Order (*rta*), does not deny the material world, or even deny that the material world exists as ultimate reality. The material world is a reality that the worshiper must contend with but must somehow also overcome. That journey is made though the multiple levels of the Vedic universe. It constitutes the necessary starting point where the worshiper begins the spiritual quest and is the path from which informs the worshiper's spiritual journey. This explains the quote cite in the previous rc (mantra) from the Vaisesika Sutras that enlightenment and understanding obtained from the Natural Order (*rta*).

These possible universes are based on the Vedic cardinal numbers.

There are four cardinal numbers in the Vedic universe. The four cardinal numbers are Two, Three, Five and Seven. These cardinal numbers are subsumed in and are most completely reflected in the Vedic force/

deity, Agni, the Principle of Change and Transformation. Agni expressly subsumes three of those cardinal points and accomplishes the world yajna in five movements, three and seven threads. (RV 10.52.4.) These numbers are the coordinates which are incorporated into the structure of the universe. The microcosm and macrocosm are interpreted with reference to these cardinal numbers. These cardinal numbers or points more importantly correspond and relate to the multi-universes in the structure of dharma, the Natural Order (*rta*). These multi-universes correspond to the different levels of being:

- The Two-Dimensional Universe consists of the polarities underlying in the substratum of the material world.
- The Three-Dimensional Universe unites the polar opposites present in the Two-Dimensional Universe.
- The subtle basis of the Three-Dimensional Universe is refined in the Five-Dimensional Universe.
- The transcendent world beyond the strictures of time and space are found in the Seven-Dimensional Universe. This level is the very core of the Vedic dharma.

In modern physics parallel universes are theories, but in the Vedas, they are a reality. Instead of searching deeper and deeper into the structure of matter, these parallel multi-universes are, yes, to be found in physical matter. But the Vedic multi-universes are also to be found in the relationship with the consciousness that perceives them. Both physically and mentally, the worshiper traverses upward to higher planes through intense meditation and concentration.

The necessary element of the Vedic divine dynamic cosmic order (*rta*) is the material universe wherein we all live. Once the Purusa, the consciousness of the macrocosm and microcosm, appears, the universe and all its forms, is created. On one level, the macrocosm and microcosm are the divine dynamic cosmic order (*rta*). The Vedic dharma (*rta*) includes both the material and the subtle worlds. Collectively it is known in the Sanskrit as loka, "the world."

In the beginning this element of the Vedic dharma was inert physical matter. Samkhya Karika 1.20 teaches us that consciousness appears in the world when Purusa, the universal consciousness, makes contact, "conjoins," with Prakrti, primordial, inert, matter. In the Veda this conjoining is symbolized in the battle between Indra and Vrtra. ((RV 1.36.8; 1.52.8; 1.80.5; 1.51.4; 1.85.9; 1.32.10; 1.52.6; 1.56.6; 1.80.3; 1.174.2; 2.4.2; 2.20.7; 3.32.6; 3.45.2; 6.20.6; 6.72.3; 8.33.1; 8.96.18; 8.6.13; 8.76.3; 8.89.4, 5, 17; 10.66.8.)

Indra's victory over Vrtra creates the next element of *rta*, that Natural Order. In this aspect the inert matter of the Two-Dimensional Universe makes a quantum leap, via the Three-Dimensional Universe, to the subtle basis of that world, the Five-Dimensional Universe, thereby imbuing the world with consciousness. This transformation is expressed in many ways:

- Consistent with the Principle of Increase, Indra released the streams after slaying Vrtra. (RV 1.33.13; 1.51.11; 1.80.10; 2.28.4; 3.31.11, 16; 4.18.7; 4.19.8; 5.30.10.) Vrtra retained the waters (RV 1.55.5; 1.57.6; 5.32.2; 5.33.1), releasing the waters. (RV 6.20.2.) The waters were set free. (RV 1.32.4.) The waters are that aspect of the Vedic dharma symbolizing the forces of creation, purification and life.

- The releasing of the waters gives birth to the hiranyabarbha, the cosmic egg. (RV 10.121.7, 8.)

- Indra is apsuji, the beloved conqueror of the waters. (RV 8.13.2; 8.36.1 - 6; 8.43.28; 9.106.3.)

- Indra released the seven rivers. (RV 1.32.12; 2.12.3; 10.67.12.) The seven rivers hold especial significance to the Vedic dharma (*rta*). The seven rivers represent the seven-dimensional, transcendent, world.

- Asat (non-being, non-existence, anti-matter) is converted into sat (being, existence, matter). (RV 6.24.5.) In other words by conquering Vrtra Indra gives the spark of existence to dead, inert matter. This is not surprising because that very essence of life is symbolized by the Waters, which Indra also set free.

Let's be clear on the dynamics of this interplay. There are three elements in this aspect to the Vedic dharma (*rta*). The first element is Indra. Indra is the Vedic force which represents the energy of light. Indra belongs to the same etymological group for "kindle," indhate (RV 1.22.21; 1.36.4, 7; 1.170.4; 2.35.11; 3.10.1, 9; 3.13.5; 3.27.11; 4.8.5; 5.7.2; 6.2.3; 6.16.48; 7.16.4; 8.43.27; 8.45.1; 8.60.15; 10.69.1), to kindle, to start a fire. The kindling refers to that which ignites the process of creation in physical matter. Indra is of the light of consciousness obtained through knowledge. Indra is important to the Vedic dharma:

- Indra is the kindling is that ignites the force of consciousness.
- Indra represents the spark of this energy of consciousness.
- As a matter of physical properties, Indra represents pure Energy.

The second element is Indra's instrument, Vajra. (RV 1.11.1; 1.7.2; 1.32.1; 1.40.8; 1.52.5; 1.103.4; 1.130.3; 4.20.2; 5.30.1; 6.18.6; 6.29.3; 7.34.4; 7.49.1; 8.1.8; 8.33.4; 8.66.4; 8.97.13; 10.56.7.) Vajra is Indra's weapon, it is also the lightning and thunder Indra's weapon releases, it is the brilliance that emanates from Indra's weapon. It is the medium by which the Energy in Indra is communicated.

The third element is Vrtra, Indra's adversary. The name of Vrtra is derived from the Sanskrit root meaning a covering, and etymologically, Vrtra is a derivation of *rta*, the Vedic dharma: V + Rta = Vrtra. Vrtra, indeed, is the "enveloper" and conceals access to and the knowledge of the Vedic dharma, *rta*, covering the true nature of the Vedic dharma with the mistaken notion that the visible world is the true reality. Vrtra can be viewed as a fallen angel of sorts, because while the serpent originally is of divine origin, its purpose is to conceal and deceive. Vrtra is the outer sheath of the Vedic dharma and its function is to cover and conceal the inner truth from humanity. The veil of Vrtra is lifted over the Vedic dharma (*rta*) when Indra's weapon, Vajra, makes contract and vanquishes Vrtra. This is the discreet moment when the inert matter (Prakrti) is converted to the living breathing material world.

When Indra emerges victorious over Vrtra with his instrument Vajra, the world and all things in the world are articulated (SA, 5.4): As the principle of Increase, Indra is the maker of forms. (RV 1.4.1; SV 160; SV 1087.) More precisely, Indra is the active Vedic force and principle for the articulation of mind and matter. Indra, in his manifestation as the Maker of Forms performs these functions:

- Deposits all names.
- Deposits all smell and odors.
- Deposits all forms.
- Deposits all sounds.
- Deposits all mind and thoughts.

The word Vajra is just one of many synonyms in the Veda for "light." Vajra is metaphorical for the power of the divine light. For example, vajra is frequently described as "brilliant." (RV 2.11.4.) Vajra is not simple light, but brilliant light, adamantine, laser-bright, and with his sword of light Indra defeats Vrtra, literally shining a light in the darkness. Appropriately enough, with the demise of Vrtra,

- The darkness is scattered. (RV 5.31.3.)
- A path is cut through the darkness to the Sun. (RV 6.21.3.)
- Indra releases or gives humanity the light, or truth. (RV 1.42.2; 1.100.8; 2.12.3; 2.11.18; 2.14.3; 2.21.4; 2.24.3, 6; 3.30.14, 20, 21; 3.34.4.; 3.38.7; 3.39.7; 4.19.7; 4.22.5, 10; 5.42.18; 8.45.19.)

"Three Wheels"

This portion concerns the Vedic Three-Dimensional Universe of the Vedic dharma (*rta*).

The Three-Dimensional Universe integrates the worshiper to the physical world after beginning the Vedic path to salvation. While the Two-Dimensional Universe is considered the vehicle of motion in the material universe, the Three-Dimensional Universe *is* that motion. The Three-Dimensional Universe is a vehicle by which the opposites inherent in the Two-Dimensional Universe are conjoined and coalesce. The act of uniting and conjoining the polar opposites of the Two-Dimensional Universe creates the material world of height, length, and breadth.

The Three-Dimensional Universe plays an important part in the Vedic path to salvation. While for the purposes of the Eternal Law of Creation, this triad is the first step to the worshiper's integration with the universe. In the Eternal Law of Salvation and Purification, the ability to conjoin and unite opposites is a prime instrument for the worshiper's salivation and an ability the worshiper will use for the remainder of the journey to liberation.

The triads of the Three-Dimension universe is consistent with the totality of Existence. There are three regions in the Vedic dharma. There is the upper, unmanifested, higher, world, known as Avyakta. Below is the lower world level of sensible appearance, referred to as Vyahrti. Between the sensible and unmanifested there lies the sun world of the svar. This portion of the Vedic dharma is set out in the chart on the next page.

Three Tiers of the Universe
Un-manifest (Avyakta)
Svar
Manifest (Vyahrti)

The Lagadha Vedanga Jyotisa speaks of the "Rule of Three." (R - VJ, 24; Y - VJ, 42.) This is a rule of interpretation in the form of a dialectic. It takes three known aspects of a phenomenon and discovers a fourth, hitherto unknown, fact concerning that phenomenon. This rule supplements the concept of trivrt, the triplicate nature of all things, which is referenced in the Vedas. (RV 1.34.9, 12; 1.47.2; 1.118.2; 1.40.2; 8.72.8; 8.85.8; 9.86.32; 10.52.4; 10.124.1; TS 1.8.13; 2.2.5; 4.3.2; 4.4.12; 6.2.3;6.3.3.)

The "Rule of Three" reflects the Three-Dimensional Universe and the triple knowledge. (JUB, 1.1.1 - 5.) The Jaiminiya Upanishad Brahmana constructs the following correspondence for this triple knowledge:

Bhu	RgVeda	Earth
Bhuvah	Yajurveda	Atmosphere
Svar	Samaveda	Sky

The Jaiminiya Upanishad Brahmana indicates that OM is the repository of this correspondence. (JUB 1.1.6,7.) The inner meaning of this triple knowledge in this correspondence is reposed in OM. (JUB 1.2.2.) The correspondence is raised to an additional level. Once the sensible world is established, the three levels of the world are presided by different divine dynamic forces on the next page:

Earth	Agni
Atmosphere	Vayu
Sky	Sun

The different levels of the Vedic dharma (*rta*) are represented in speech. (JUB 1.2.1, 2.) It is only through speech that the articulation of names is obtained (SA, 5.4), and thereby making the sensible world intelligible. The Jaiminiya Upanishad Brahmana states that the Principle of Change (Agni) is speech and speech is the earth and that Change, and the other emanations of the Three-Dimensional Universe are reposed in OM. (JUB 1.2.1- 8.) The fire of the Principle of Change (Agni), or pervasion of consciousness, reaches to the three levels of the sensible universe:

- The sensible universe, vyahrti, consisting of bhuh, the lower world.
- Antarikstra, the mid-world, sometimes called bhuvah, the upper world; and
- Svar, the sun-world, bindu, is the hub, the gateway, the vortex which inverts and turns the sensible world on its head to tridhaatu, or mahii, the upper three levels of the world beyond the manifest universe.

The Principle of Change (Agni) pervades the sensible universe, the vyahrti. The Three-Dimensional Universe holds special significance to the Principle of Change (Agni):

- The Principle of Change (Agni) has a three-fold nature. (RV 1.95.3; 4.1.7.)
- This three-fold nature has sometimes been referred to as the "three brothers." (RV 1.164.1; 10.51.6.)
- The Principle of Change (Agni) is represented by the three altars, the Garhapatya, Ayhavaniya, and Daksina.
- The divine fashioned the Principle of Change (Agni) to have this three-fold nature. (RV 10.88.10.)
- The Principle of Change (Agni) has three heads (RV 1.146.1), residing in three stations, tongue or bodies. (RV 3.20.2.)

- The Principle of Change (Agni) resides in three abodes (RV 8.39.8), meaning heaven, earth and water. (RV 8.44.16; 10.2.7; 4.6.9.)
- The Principle of Change (Agni) is lit with three kindlings. (RV 3.2.9; 3.26.7.)

  "Kindling" in this sense should be properly understood. Physical fire is "ignited," but the Sacrificial Fire is "kindled." Kindling imparts all those qualities and energies from the universe and channeled those qualities and energies into the Fire. Specific benefits accrue to the worshiper when Agni the Sacrificial Fire is kindled. The Sacrificial Fire summons the other Vedic energies and forces and once summoned communicates those energies and forces to the worshiper. (RV 6.14.2.) The Sacrificial Fire is the spark which ignites the spiritual awakening of the worshiper. (RV 3.19.5.) The Sacrificial Fire gives the spiritual impulsions to the worshiper. (RV 3.23.2.) The impulsions are anything which propel the communication of the essential qualities of the Vedic divine forces to the worshiper.

- The Principle of Change (Agni) has three births (RV 1.95.3; 4.1.7), the first from heaven, the second from men, and the third from the waters. (RV 10.45.1.)
- There are three types of sacrificial fires associated with the Principle of Change, the Garhapatya, ayhavaniya, and daksina.

There is another aspect to the Three-Dimensional Universe. Whereas Agni in his manifestation as the Principle of Change controls the general pervasion of the Vedic dharma, Indra has a more specific function in the restraint of senses.

"The Yoked Horse"

Enfolding and encompassing the Way of Ying and Yang
Is like being an artisan and charioteer
Who level the marking-cord and the plumb-line,
Hold the bit and bridle,
Align the compass and the square
And follow the tracks and the ruts.

Cantong qi: 1.2:1 - 6.
The Seal of the Unity of Three,
Pregadio, trans.

The portion pertains to a specific type of knowledge. It speaks of a team of horses "yoking" the three wheels. That the horses yoke the wheels, instead of the other way around, is counter-intuitive. This simile is supported by an entire body of Vedic literature, categorized by what this humbler interpreter calls the Equine Knowledge. Equine Knowledge is best stated in the Katha Upanishad. (Kath. U., 3.3 - 10.) In that passage, the Katha Upanishad states:

Know the Self to be sitting in the chariot, the body to be the chariot, the intellect (Buddhi) the charioteer, and the mind the reins.

> The senses they call the horses,
> the objects of the senses their roads.
> When he (the Highest Self) is in union with the body, the senses, and the mind,
> then wise people call him the Enjoyer
> He who has no understanding and whose mind (the reins) is never firmly held, his senses (horses) are unmanageable, like vicious horses of a charioteer.
> But he who has understanding and whose mind is always firmly held,
> his senses are under control, like good horses of a charioteer.
> He who has no understanding, who is unmindful and always impure,
> never reaches that place but enters into the round of births.
>
> But he who has understanding, who is mindful and always pure,
> reaches indeed that place, from whence he is not born again.
>
> But he who has understanding for his charioteer,

and who holds the reins of the mind, he reaches the end
of his journey,
and that is the highest place of Vishnu.

Beyond the senses there are the objects, beyond the objects
there is the mind,
beyond the mind there is the intellect, the Great Self is
beyond the intellect.

This highly influential passage accomplishes much to the esoteric understanding of the symbol of the horse and its place in its cosmological structure. It delineates the various elements within which the consciousness resides:

The Self, the subject, sits with the charioteer.

The Chariot is the body.

The intellect (Buddhi) is the charioteer.

The mind, Manas, is the reins.

The senses, the indriam, are the horses.

The object of the senses is the road.

So is the image of the horse in the Veda. Equine Knowledge is the knowledge of restraint of mind. This passage from the Katha Upanishad defines the esoteric meaning of horses in the Veda. Horses in the Veda has the metaphorical meaning of the "senses," sight, touch, hear, smell, and feel. Horses represent the senses, the mind's perception of the senses, in all their unbridled glory.

There is another level to this esoteric meaning. When the worshiper perceives the surrounding world, that sense data creates a mental impression on the worshiper's mind. This mental impression is the vrttis the restraint of which Patanjali in his Yoga Sutras makes the ultimate goal in yoga. Just as once a thumb is lifted from a clump of dough and leaves a dent, these mental impressions remain long after its mental activity ceases. These mental impressions may include any number of mental activities — perceiving the sensible world, feeling happy, sad, joyous, depressed, the memories, hearing a tune in your head that you heard earlier in the day and which you liked. All these mental events are impressions lodged in the consciousness. The object of yoga is not to eliminate the vrttis; the worshiper would be brain-dead if the mental impressions were eliminated. The goal is to manage the vrttis, to restrain them, such that they are not an impediment to the spiritual or mental growth of the worshiper.

This is where Equine Knowledge enters the picture. The passage from the Katha Upanishads emphasizes the consequences of and need to yoke — i.e., restrain, control — the senses and vrttis, metaphorically represented by horses, to achieve liberation and salvation. "Yoked horses" thus becomes a metaphor for the yogic practice of pratyahara, withdrawal of senses and the organs of sense perception creating the mental impressions in the worshiper's mind.

To properly grasp the dynamics involved in perceiving, processing, and ultimate restraint the information obtained by the sense organs, recourse of the process of evolution and dissolution according to Samkhya must understood. In a nutshell, there is a process:

- When Purusa, the universal consciousness, makes contact, "conjoins," with Prakrti, primordial, inert, matter, consciousness appears in the world. (S.K., 20.)
- From Prakrti arises Mahat (S.K., 22), otherwise known as Buddhi. (S.K., 23.)

This is also one of the principal functions of the Vedic dynamism of Indra. The Mahat or Buddhi is the first principle of individualization, wherein resides the individual intellect, will, judgment, the faculty which directs awareness out into the objects of the world. In the context of the Eternal Law of Increase, Indra is the active, dynamic Vedic force representing Mahat, Buddhi. That Indra as the Buddhi is known through several epithets:

- Shakra, The Mighty. (RV 1.10.6; 5.34.3; 6.47.11; 7.104.20, 8.1.19; 8.32.12; 8.50.1;8.69.14; 8..78.5; 8.93.18; 10.43.6; 10.104.10; 10.167.2; SV 1.1.140.)
- Maghavann, the "Victor." (RV 1.23.3; 2.32.13; 11.55.5;1.73.5; 1.77.4; 1.98.3; 1.103.2, 4; 1.136.7; 1.141.13; 1.146.5; 1.157.3; 1.171.3, 5; 1.174.1, 7; 2.6.4; 3.30.3, 22; 3.31.22; 3.32.7; 3.34.11; 3.51.11; 3.36.11; 3.38.10; 3.39.9; 3.43.8; 3.48.5; 3.49.5; 3.50.5; 3.51.1; 3.53.8; 4.16.1; 4.17.8, 9, 11, 13; 4.20.2; 4.22.1; 4.24.2; 4.27.5; 4.31.7; 5.31.1; 5.34.2, 3, 8; 5.42.8; 5.61.11; 5.79.6; 6.24.1; 6.27.8; 6.47.11; 6.58.4; 7.16.7; 7.20.10; 7.21.10; 7.26.1, 2; 7.27.4; 7.28.5; 7.29.5; 7.30.3; 7.31.4; 7.32.12, 20; 7.60.11; 7.29.5; 7.30.3; 7.31.4; 8.1.12; 8.21.10; 8.26.7; 8.33.9; 8, 13; 8.46.13; 8.49.1; 8.52.5; 8.61.1, 18; 8.65.10;8.70.15; 8.95.20; 8.96.20; 8.97.13; 8.103.9; 9.81.3; 9.96.11; 9.97.55; 10.23.2, 3; 10.10.27.4; 10.33.8; 10.42.6, 8; 10.43.1, 3, 5, 6, 8; 10.49.11; 10.74.5; 10.81.6; 10.89.18; 10.104.11; 10.113.2; 10.160.4; 10.162.2.)
- Shatakratu, the Possessor of Many Powers. (RV 8.93.16.)
- Satraaji, the Perpetual Lord. (RV 8.3.15; 9.89.4; 9.27.4.)
- Mahan, the Mighty.

Having established the faculty by which the sense information surrounding the worshiper may be processed, the process of evolution proceeds:

- From Mahat, the individual ego, Ahamkara, emerges. (S.K., 22.)
- From the ego, Manas, the mind, and the attributes and qualities of contained in the sense objects, arise. (S.K., 22, 24.)

It is at this stage that the mind of the worshiper can perceive all that around it in the world. In summary:

- Indra becomes the Buddhi.
- Restraint or yoking of the horses becomes Pratyahara.
- The horses to be yoked are the mental impressions (vrttis) of the mind.

Yoking the horses (union) is the stated goal of yoga. Horses are frequently associated with the Vedic divine dynamic forces:

- The horse is associated with the processes of the Principle of Change (Agni) through metaphor and simile. (RV 3.27.14; 3.29.6; 6.3.4; 8.22; 4.2.8; 1.36.8; 1.27.1; 1.6.53; 1.66.2; 1.69.3; 1.73.9, 10; 1.74.7; 1.149.3; 1.58.2; 2.1.16; .2.2.10; 3.2.3; 3.26.3; 4.1.3; 4.2.4.4.39.6; 4.2.11; 4.10.1; 4.15.1; 5.6.3; 5.18.5.)
- Usas, mental and spiritual awareness, is seen mounting the carriage as the charioteer (the Self). (RV 3.61.2.)
- Owing to their extremely concentrated focus, the Maruts move with swift horses (senses) which are easily controlled. (RV 5.55.1; 5.54.1.)

The Horses (sense perceptions) however are ruled and governed by other aspects. For example, the senses (horses) are harnessed in accordance with the dynamic force of *rta*. (RV 4.51.5.) The horse is primarily used as a metaphor for the senses, consistent with the interpretation given in the Katha Upanishad:

- The Soma plant is ground with the pistol and mortar much like reins are used to tether a horse. (RV 1.28.4.)
- Varuna (Lord Protector of the Dynamic Cosmic Order)'s mind, and by extension our own, are soothed by the praises at the sacrifice like the horses (sense perceptions) are soothed by the reins (mind). (RV 1.25.3.)
- The worshiper accepts the offering as a charioteer (the Self) accepts the reins (mind) to a horse (senses). (RV 1.144.3.)

The dynamic Vedic forces each possess their own horses which the Brhad-Devata (BD, 4.140, 141) list as the following:

- The Bay Horses (Hari), the horses of Indra. (Nir., 1.15.1.)
- The Ruddy Ones (rohit), the horses of Agni.
- Fallows (harit), the horses of Surya.
- Teams (niyut), the horses of Vayu.
- The Ass (sahita), the horses of the Asvins.

- The Steeds (vajin), the horses of Pusan.
- The Drappled mares (prsati), the horses of the Maruts.
- The Ruddy Cows (aruni), the horses of Usas, Dawn.

Each steed represents a different aspect of the mind-body relationship, and each have its own specific quality regarding their respective dynamic Vedic force. In Hari, for instance, the horses of Indra, is the instrument of achieving divine inspiration, ecstacy and union. In reaching that goal, constant mention is made to "harness the horses" so that they may be "yoked." This is but another way of saying that the mind must be restrained, controlled, and focused to achieve liberation and salvation. In this aspect Indra acts as the Lord of the sense perceptions. Indra acts as a true Lord, one which exercises mastery to restrain and calm the mind which perceives the sense data. The dynamic force of knowledge and discernment (Indra), appropriately, plays a central role in the riding (restraint) of the horses (sense perceptions):

- The dynamic force of Knowledge (Indra), appropriately, is called the "Lord of the Bay (Horses), consistent with the need of knowledge to restrain the fluctuations of sense perceptions. (RV 1.3.6; 1.33.6; 1.81.4; 1.145.3; 1.147.1; 1.173.13; 1.174.6; 1.175.1; 3.30.2; 3.32.5; 3.47.4; 3.51.6; 3.52.7;4.16.21; 4.17.21; 4.19.11; 4.20.11; 4.21.11; 4.22.11; 4.23.11; 4.24.11; 4.35.7; 5.31.2; 6.19.6; 6.32.3; 6.41.3; 6.44.10; 7.19.4, 7;7.20.4; 7.21.1; 7.23.4; 7.24.4, 5; 7.29.1; 7.32.12; 7.37.4, 5; 8.2.13; 8.21.6; 8.24.3, 5, 14; 8.40.9; 8.48.10; 8.50.3; 8.55.4; 8.88.2; 10.49.11.)
- The dynamic force of the Buddhi (Indra) is the "yoker" of the Bay Horses. (RV 1.6.2; 1.82.1, 2; 1.61.16; 1.81.3; 1.82.3, 4, 5; 1.83.3; 1.141.6; 3.43.6; 5.40.4; 6.23.1; 6.37.1; 6.47.18, `19; 7.28.1; 8.3.17; 8.33.14; 8.45.39; 8.59.7; 8.79.3, 9; 10.33.5; 10.105.2; 10.122.4.)
- The dynamic force of knowledge and discernment (Indra) yokes, or restrains, the fluctuations of the senses. (RV 3.50.2.)
- The movement of the dynamic force of knowledge and discernment (Indra) in the chariot (body) thus becomes the seat of discernment. (RV 3.53.6.)

Other themes emerge:

- Indra (Buddhi) yokes (restrains) the horses (senses/vrttis). (RV 1.5.4; 1.6.4; 1.84.6; 1.161.6, 21; 5.33.2; 7.19.6; 10.23.1, 3; 10.44.2; 10.105.5.)
- The horses (senses/vrttis) yoked (restrained) by prayer. (RV 1.28.7; 1.82.6; 1.84.3; 2.18.7; 3.35.4; 4.32.15; 8.2.27; 8.17.2; 8.45.39.)
- Hari (the organs of sense perceptions) bring Indra (Buddhi) to the sacrifice. (RV 1.82.1; 3.35.2; 3.43.4; 8.12.15; 10.23.2.)
- The sacrifice is a journey, the journey of the worshiper's soul. In this way the harnessed horses (restrained senses/vrttis) transport the worshiper on that journey. (RV 2.18.2.)
- Indra (Buddhi) yokes (restrains) Hari (the sense organs/vrttis) to battle the enemies, metaphorical for confronting evil, ignorance, or anything else which might retard progress in the Vedic path to liberation and salvation. (RV 1.81.3; 6.57.3.)
- Principal among the enemies is Vrtra, and the horses (senses/vrttis) must be yoked (restrained) to fight against Vrtra (ignorance). (RV 8.3.17; 8.12.25, 26, 27; 8.12.25.)
- Hari (the organs of sense perceptions/vrttis) bring Indra (Buddhi) to the sacrifice to drink Soma (divine ecstacy). (RV 1.10.3; 1.16.21; 1.55.7; 1.82.5; 1.177.4; 3.35.1; 5.43.5; 6.40.1; 8.3.17; 8.6.45; 8.13.31; 8.14.12; 8.32.30; 10.96.6; 10.160.1.) Symbolically, this signifies that restrained mind is one of the means to achieve self-realization.
- Hari (the organs of sense perceptions/vrttis) bring Indra (Buddhi) to the sacrifice to eat food. (RV 1.82.2, 3, 4.)
- The horses (senses/vrttis) must be yoked (restrained) to receive the benefits of the sacrifice. (RV 1.82.1, 3.)

Related to this is the "unyoking" of the horses/vrttis. Soma, the divine dynamic energy and the elixir, is a significant participant in the unyoking. Consider:

- The dynamic Vedic energy of divine union (Soma) acts to "unyoke" the horses. (RV 3.32.1.) This is the nature of the ecstacy of divine union. After the experience — any experience — of divine union, the worshiper's perception of the world is different. Instead of viewing the world in black and white, the world is suddenly, as in the Wizard of Oz, in living color. The worshiper experiences what Alan Watts states any seeker must do — get "out of your mind." In the language of the Veda, the horses are unyoked.

- Thus, when the experience of divine union is experienced after consumption of the Soma juice at the sacrifice, the senses flow, like Soma, like a rapid horse. (RV 9.16.1; 9.23.2; 9.26.1; 9.36.1; 9.59.1; 9.62.6; 9.72.1; 9.74.1; 9.93.1; 9.96.20; 9.97.18; 9.101.2.)

In the journey on the Vedic path to salvation and liberation the worshiper strives to keep the senses under control, learn to restrain the mind and manage the mental impressions (vrttis). If that skill is mastered, the worshiper will not be not subject to rebirth. If not, if the worshiper's mind is unrestrained, a "monkey mind," if the senses are not in control, the worshiper will be subject to constant re-birth time after time.

"The Horse Has Seven Names."

No, this is not a horse with no name; it is a horse with Seven names. This portion of the rc (mantra) implicates the Seven–Dimension universe. This is the topic more fully discussed in the next rc. If the horses represent the vrttis which need to be restrained or yoked to achieve higher consciousness, the horse with "seven names" is that higher consciousness. This rc (mantra) demonstrates the expanse and plenum of Vedic dharma, the Natural Order (*rta*). There exists not just the material world of sensory perceptions but subtler reflections of this world. And notice the directions these multiple universes take.

- The Two-Dimensional Universe is that everyday world we all live in.
- In the Three-Dimensional Universe the movement of the everyday world is tuned inward and the essential elements of that world are revealed.
- Those elements are further defined and articulated in the Five-Dimensional Universe.

- Once the Worshiper begins to realize the Seven-Dimensional Universe that consciousness is turned ever inward and out again, to define the Worshiper's inner world and beyond.

The Seven-Dimension Universe represents transcendence, and this transcendence is the principal characteristic of Vedic dharma, the Natural Order (*rta*). Transcendence has both macrocosmic, microcosmic, and personal aspects. In a macrocosmic aspect, the bounds of this material world are transcended beyond to the heavens. In a microcosmic aspect consist of the subtle, sub-atomic boundaries of matter. On a personal level, the worshiper achieves liberation. The precise boundaries of the Seven-Dimensional Universe continue in the next rc.

RV 1.164.3:

The seven horses carry the seven sisters
who have the "seven utterances."

A MODEST INTERPRETATION:

The last cardinal number in the Vedic dharma is Seven. The Seven-Dimensional Universe is that transcendent world beyond the confines of time and space.

This rc (mantra) is a reference to the cardinal number Seven. The Seven-Dimensional Universe is an extension of the cardinal number Seven. The number Seven holds special significance in the Rg Veda; that significance originates from the Seven-Dimensional Universe and the presence it holds in establishing the macrocosm and microcosm.

The number Seven has a universal appeal. According to the ancients, the number Seven, the heptad, is "not born of any mother and is a virgin." This means the number Seven is a part of the uncreated, the unborn, outside the realm of becoming, and resides in the realm of Pure Being. This applies as well to all that is associated or consists of the heptad. Iamblichus expressly mentions the seven planets, the seven directions, the seven modes of movement, the soul, the seven vowels, the seven ages, the seven seasons, and other associations. Because it is uncreated and belongs to the realm of unchanging Being, there is a divine element to the heptad.

The Greek philosopher Iamblichus also makes mention of the seven "alterations of voice." (*The Theology of Arithmetic*, Waterfield, trans., (1988), p. 87.) This reflects the Sama Chant in the Vedas, which consists of Himkara,

Prastava, Adi, Ugditha, Pratihara, Upadrava, and Nidhana. There is also a bhakti tradition of five aspirations of breath in the Sama chant; this tradition omits Adi and Upadrava. The seven bhakti makes a more complete cycle.

Creation is ruled by heptads. Sayana interprets the seven horses and seven sisters in terms of time periods and seasons. This modest interpretation is more expansive, encompassing the sensible and subtle worlds. Sayana interprets the "seven utterances" as the seven notes of the Saman chant. These notes, when uttered at the sacrifice, represent prana, the undulations of the dynamic rhythm of the universe. These notes are the Logos, the phonetic expression of *rta*, the Word.

In the Veda, the Seven-Dimensional Universe represents the macrocosm of the Vedic dharma, *rta*. Just as a transcendent world must have a point of reference from which the worshiper is transcended, this macrocosm is viewed against the Three-Dimensional Universe. This is because Vedic cosmology is based on an over-arching system of triads, where everything in the universe is manifested in triplicate (trivrt). (Sank.Br., 7.2 - 6.) This triplicate nature is found in every subdivision of the various levels of the Vedic dharma.

The Seven-Dimensional Universe is grounded in the transcendent, spiritual world. In recognition that the transcendent world implicates the material world, there are seven levels, incorporating both the material and transcendent levels.

In the beginning stages of creation, described in RV 10.190, Satyam and *Rta* are found at the highest level of Being. (RV 10.190.1.) RV 6.24.5 relates that when Indra felled Vrtra with Vayra, he divided the world into two parts: one part, "What is," and the other, "What is not." The forces of Indra and Soma cast "What is not" below the triple structure of the world. (RV 7.104.11.) What remains is "What is." From there, Rta and Satya emerge. Of the two, *Rta* prevails over and pervades satyam. As Hickman notes in his "*Toward a Comprehensive Understanding of Rta in the Rg Veda*," Satya is "being" manifested by the establishment of the universe, but *Rta* is the mode of that being which promotes and supports the freedom and mobility of satyam. The former, *rta*, furnishes the framework for the latter, satya, and allows it as well as all other subjects in the cosmic order to function. *Rta* is the internal mechanism of the proverbial watch which regulates the ticking of the universe. Satyam and *Rta* create the second highest level of being, Tapas. (RV 10.190.1.) After Tapas, Madhuunaam, or Bliss, is the bottom tier of the higher world. In the Atharveda, those highest stations are *Rta*, Satyam and Brhat (the Vast). (AV 12.1.1.)

The Seven-Dimensional is a combination of the three upper and three lower levels of existence, conjoined together by the Svar. There are three levels of sensible appearance, the earth, mid-world, and heaven. (RV 1.34.7; 1.154.4.) In some passages, these lower three regions have been referred to as "tridhaatu prthhvim," (RV 1.34.7; 1.154.4) which can be roughly rendered as the "three levels of the material plane."

Each level contains three subdivisions. There are three levels of heaven, dyaus. (RV 1.35.6; AV 8.9.16.) The three divisions of heaven are:

- uttama(m) (RV 1.24.15; 1.25.21; 1.50.10; 1.91.8; 1.108.9; 1.156.4; 1.163.7; 2.1.2; 2.23.10; 3.5.6, 8; 4.315; 436.8; 4.54.2; 5.25.5; 5.28.3; 5.59.3; 9..22.6; 9.51.2; 9.63.29; 9.67.3, 28; 9.85.3; 9.107.1; 9.108.16; 10.75.1; 10.97.18; 10.159.3; 10.166.5; 10.78.3), or uttame. (RV 1.31.7; 2.41.5; 5.60.4; 6.60.3, 8; 8.51.4; 9.61.29.)
- madhyama (RV 1.24.15; 1.25.21; 1.108.9, 10; 2.29.4; 4.25.8; 6.21.5; 6.62.11; 7.32.16; 8.61.15;9.70.4; 9.108.9; 10.15.1; 10.81.5; 10.97.12) or madhyame (RV 1.27.5; 2.23.13; 5.60.6; 6.25.1) and
- avama or avame. (RV 1.105.4; 1.108.9, 10; 1.163.5; 2.35.2; 3.54.5; 6.251; 6.62.11; 7.71.3; 1.185.11.)

There are also three levels of heaven in the Atharva Veda. The highest level is that level where the ptrs (fathers) and angirasas reside. (AV 18.2.12, 48.) The second level is the "starry" heaven (AV 18.2.12, 48), and the third, lowest, level is the "watery" heaven. (AV 18.2.12, 48.) Elsewhere in the Vedas, there are three levels to the atmosphere, the mid-world, firmament; there are three levels to the lowest level of the material world. (RV 1.34.8; AV 8.9.16.)

The three aspects of the Principle of Change and Transformation, Agni, Jatavedas, and Vasivanara, embody the lower three regions. (BD, 1.6.6.) Agne is the embodiment of the earth, and Jatadevas is the embodiment of the mid-earth. (RV 1.77.5; 2.4.1; 3.1.20; 4.1.20; 4.58.8; 6.4.2; 6.10.1; 6.12.4; 6.15.13; 7.9.4; 7.12.2; 10.45.1; 10.61.14; 10.83.2; 10.88.4.) Vasivanara is the embodiment of heaven. (RV 1.59.3, 4, 6, 7; 1.98.1, 2; 3.2.1, 11, 12; 3.3.1, 5, 11; 3.26.1, 2, 3; 4.5.1, 2; 5.15.13; 6.7.1, 2, 6, 7; 6.8.1, 2, 3, 4; 6.9.1, 7; 7.5.1, 2, 5; 7.6.6, 7; 7.13.1; 7.49.4; 8.30.4; 9.61.16; 10.45.12; 10.88.12, 13, 14.) Indra, in his representation of strength and vitality, embodies the mid-world. The Purified Mind (Soma), the inherence of the Eternal Law of God-Realization and Purification, embodies heaven.

The two levels of existence are bound together by the Svar. The Svar is the transitory world of heaven and light. The svar, is an intermediate world of heaven and light. (RV 1.35.6.) There are three subdivisions to each region, and each have three subdivisions. (RV 3.56.8.) Light is another element to this structure. There are three regions of light in the svar. Those regions are called rocana, svar, and rajastui (rajastu). (RV 1.102.7; 2.27.9; 1.149.4; 4.33.5; 5.29.1; 5.69.1; 9.17.5.) There are also regions of light. (RV 1.102.7; 1.149.4; 3.56.8; 4.53.5; 5.69.1; 5.29.1; 9.17.5.) Those three regions of light are:

- Rocana. (RV 1.49.1; 1.49.4; 1.50.4; 1.81.5; 1.93.5; 1.102.8; 1.146.1; 1.149.4; 2.27.9; 3.2.14; 3.5.10; 3.12.9; 3.44.4; 3.56.8; 3.61.5; 4.53.5; 3.61.5; 5.29.1; 5.56.1; 5.61.1; 5.69.4; 6.6.2; 6.7.7; 8.1.18; 8.5.8; 8.8.7; 8.14.7; 8.14.9; 8.93.26; 8.94.8; 8.98.3; 9.17.5; 9.37.3; 9.42.1; 9.85.9; 10.32.9; 10.46.3; 10.49.6; 10.65.4; 10.89.1; 10.170.4; 10.189.2.) Rocana is the highest sphere of light. (RV 1.6.1, 9; 1.19.6; 1.81.5; 1.86.1; 1.92.17; 1.113.7; 1.121.9; 1.124.3; 1.146.1; 3.2.14; 5.41.3; 6.7.7; 6.44.23; 8..1.8; 8.14.9; 8.25.19; 8.52.8; 9.42.1; 9.85.9; 9.61.10; 10.32.2; 10.70.5; 10.143.3.)
- Upannam ketu. (RV 5.34.9.)
- Svar, and Rejastui (RV 1.164.12; 6.2.2; 6.66.7; 9.84.4; 9.108.2) is also known as rajasi. (RV 1.125.20; 1.36.12; 1.188.1; 5.8.5; 5.28.2; 5.81.5; 7.32.16; 8.13.4; 8.15.3; 8.15.5; 8.19.31; 8.37.3; 8.60.15; 9.66.2; 9.86.5, 28; 10.140.4; 10.167.1.)

The Seven-Dimensional Universe is laid out in the following chart:

Seven Tiers of the Universe
rtam/Satyam
Tapas
Madhuunaam
Svar
Heaven
Mid-Earth
Earth

The number Seven refers to the seven planes of existence. (RV 1.22.6; 8.40.5; 1.114.3; 10.122.2; 6.62.12.) The number Seven is applied to a good many subjects and situations:

- The seven regions of earth. (RV 1.22.16.)
- The seven daughters or sisters (RV 1.164.3; 1.191.14 6.61.10; 6.61.12; 8.41.2, 9; 9.61.8; 9.86.36; 10.5.5) which probably refer to the Pleiades.
- The seven mothers (RV 1.141.2; 8.85.1; 9.102.4; 10.10.4; 1.34.8), representatives of the Female Principle. (RV 1.50.9; 1.141.2; 1.191.14; 6.61.10; 8.41.2; 8.85.1; 9.66.8; 9.86.36; 10.5.5.)
- The seven singers. (RV 1.62.4; 3.7.7; 1.62.4; 4.16.3; 5.43.1; 9.15.8; 9.92.2; 10.5.5; 10.71.3.)
- The seven castles which are destroyed by Indra. (RV 1.63.7; 1.174.2; 6.20.10; 7.18.13.)
- The seven rays of sunlight. (RV 1.55.9.)
- The seven sons or fathers, representing the Male Principle. (RV 1.164.1 (sons); 4.42.8.)
- The seven reins (RV 2.5.2; 2.12.2; 2.18.1; 6.44.24), which, according to Sayana, refers to the leader of the sacrifice, but according to our interpretation, related to the symbol of the Horses, are the mental and psychological reins which guide the worshiper's consciousness upwards in the spiritual ladder.
- The seven-wheeled car (RV 2.40.3) is symbolic of the macrocosm.
- The seven-priests (RV 3.4.5; 3.10.4; 3.29.14; 3.31.5; 3.4.5; 8.49.16; 9.7.4; ; 9.8.4; 9.10.7; 9.114.3; 10.3, 7; 10.35.10; 10.61.1; 10.63.7; 10.64.5), which on one level represents the ministrants at the ritual, but on a deeper level the worshiper's seven spiritual levels. Alternatively, the seven priests are symbolic of the Pleiades.
- The seven rishis (RV 3.7.7; 3.31.5; 4.2.15; 6.22.2; 9.92.2; 10.82.2; 10.109.24; 10.114.7; 10.130.7), which refer to the Vedic Seers who authored the Rg Veda, and/or the asterisms in the Vedic sky, or the Big Dipper constellation. The seven priests are symbolic of the Pleiades.
- The seven rivers, many of which are implicated with The Purified Mind (Soma)(RV 3.1.4; 3.1.6; 1.32.12; 1.34.8 ("the mother

streams"); 1.35.8; 1.71.7; 1.72.8 ("floods from heaven"); 1.100.2; 2.12.3; 2.12.12; 4.19.3; 4.38.1; 6.7.6; 7.18.24; 7.36.6; 7.67.8; 8.24.8; 8.58.12; 9.54.2; 9.61.6; 9.66.6; 9.92.4; 10.43.3; 10.49.9; 10.64.8; 10.67.12; 10.75,1; 10.104.8), also signifying the Milky Way, or the Pleiades.

- There is the seven-headed hymn. (RV 3.5.5; 8.3.4; 10.62.1.)
- The Principle of Change (Agni) is said to have the "seven-tongued flame. (RV 3.6.2; 1.58.7; 1.105.9; 1.166.1; 4.7.5; 4.50.4 (Bhraspati); 8.61.16; 9.102.2 ("the seven lights of the sacrifice"); 10.8.8.)
- The seven tones from the sacrificial viand. (RV 3.7.1; 4.51.4; 10.32.4.)
- The seven libations. (RV 1.20.7; 10.17.11; 10.25.10.)
- The seven Adityas, or solar deities. (RV 1.50.9; 4.13.3; 5.43.1; 5.45.8; 8.28.5; 1.114.3; 9.114.3.)
- The seven castles. (RV 1.63.7'; 1.114.2; 6.20.10; 7.18.3.)
- The seven-wheeled chariot (RV 1.164.2, 3, 12; 2.49.3), a likely reference to the Vedic seven-month calendar year.
- Indra, as the "seven-rayed" bull. (RV 2.12.12.)
- Trita (Aptya) killed the three-headed with seven rays. (RV 10.8.8.)
- The seven cows. (RV 1.164.3; 9.86.25; 6.44.24.)
- The seven sons. (RV 10.72.8, 9.)
- The seven heros. (RV 10.27.15.)
- The seven threads. (RV 1.164.5; 10.5.6; 10.52.4; 10.124.1.)
- The seven seeds. (RV 1.164.36.)
- The seven rains. (RV 2.12.2; 2.5.2;2.18.1; 6.44.24; 9.62.17.)
- The seven suns. (TA, 1.7.1, 3, 4.)
- The seven directions. (RV 9.114.3.)
- The seven rich treasures. (RV 5.1.5; 6.74.1 (Soma-Rudra); 8.61.16.)
- The seven rays of knowledge. (RV 1.105.9; 4.50.4 (Bhraspati); 8.61.16 (emanating from the sun); 10.8.8.)
- The seven devotions. (RV 9.9.2, 6.)
- In an interesting passage indicating its great antiquity, the Rg Veda indicates there are seven months. (RV 9.111.1.)
- Reference is also made to the seven steeds or horses, referring to the energies inherent in each level of the planes of Vedic existence. (RV 3.7.8; 1.50.8; 3.4.7; 7.61.15 (as the "the seven sisters").)

- Seven shining energies. (RV 7.60.3.)
- The seven layers of Agni, the fire altar. (SPB 6.6.6.14; 6.8.2.7; 7.3.2.1; 9.1.1.26; 9.1.2.31; 9.2.3.44, 45; 9.5.2.8.)
- The seven Invokers of the Soma juice. (RV 10.17.11; AV 18.4.12; TA 6.6.2.)
- The seven horses drawing the chariot of Surya. (RV 1.164.2; 5.45.9.) This could signify symbolically the Sun leading the other planets around their orbits.
- The Seven Samurai, The Magnificent Seven, Seven Brides for Seven Brothers, The Seven Year Itch, and the Seven Words You Can't Say on Television.

Alright, not that last entry. But you get the picture. There is a visceral, mystic ring to the number Seven which is ubiquitous in mystic or occult literature, as well as pop culture, in all cultures. The number Seven continues to have its appeal. This universal appeal is grounded on the Seven-Dimension Universe, the very space of transcendence.

There is no concept more obscure or occult, however, than the Thrice Seven Tongues of Transformation (Agni).

"Thrice Seven"

"Thrice Seven" is one of the more obscure phrases which makes frequent appearances in the Rg Veda. "Thrice Seven" combines the essential qualities of the cardinal numbers Three and Seven, incorporated in the Three- and Seven-Dimension universes. The Three-Dimensional Universe is the subtle aspect of the material world. The Seven-Dimensional Universe is the transcendent universe. "Thrice seven" is the metaphorical leap from the subtle aspect of the material world to the transcendent. In this respect "Thrice Seven" implicates the collective microcosm and macrocosm.

The concept of the "Thrice Seven," trih sapta, recurs throughout the Vedas, in the Rg Veda in several rcs (RV 1.72.6; 1.191.12, 14; 4.1.16; 7.87.4; 8.46.26; 8.96.2; 9.86.21; 10.64.8; 10.90.15) and in the Brahmanas. Its meaning is tantalizingly obscure and varied. The Brahmanas unanimously indicate that "Thrice Seven" refers to:

- 12 months,
- 5 seasons,
- 3 worlds,
- One Sun,

and further state that the Sun is the world. (TS 7.3.10; 5.4.12; AB 30.4; TB 3.8.10; KB 11.6; PB 6.2.2;SPB 1.3.5.11.) This interpretation implicates the macrocosm. It encompasses both a division of time and its assignment to the physical worlds. The occult meaning of "Thrice Seven" according to these passages could be said to include both the "spatial and temporal expanse of the physical universe" and that area beyond the spatial and temporal boundaries of the material world. In other words, the Vedic dharma.

"Thrice Seven" is an extension of the "Rule of Three" referenced in the Lagadha Vedanga Jyotisa. (RVJ, 24; YVJ, 42.) This "Rule of Three" must be viewed against the many references in the Veda of the number seven which were listed above. References of this number have been widely interpreted as representative of the seven levels of existence, both the macrocosm and microcosm, the Seven-Dimensional Universe.

There are seven levels to the macrocosm and microcosm and three different fuels impelling each level. (AV 19.6.15.) "Thrice Seven" communicates a deeper aspect of the macrocosm and microcosm. On one level it provides a cosmological framework for the transcendent Seven-Dimensional Universe where each level contains three different subdivisions. On another level it provides a mechanism whereby the worshiper can jump start from the material world to the transcendent world. This process is symbolized in the construction of the Fire Altar. The Fire Altar represents the whole world and the bricks the regions. (SPB 7.3.1.13.) The vedi, the sacrificial enclosure, represents the earth. (SPB 7.3.1.15.) Specifically, in constructing the fifth layer of the Fire Altar with Stamobhaga bricks, twenty-one bricks are used to symbolize the three worlds and the regions. (SPB 8.5.3.5, 6.) Each level of the fifth layer contains three layers and represents a different, progressively elevated, layer of the cosmic order:

- The first three layers, one through three, is symbolic of the world;

- The second three layers, four through six, is symbolic of the mid-earth;
- The third three layers, seven through nine, is symbolic of the heavens;
- The fourth three layers, ten through twelve, is symbolic of the eastern quarter;
- The fifth three layers, thirteen through fifteen, is symbolic of the southern quarter;
- The sixth three layers, sixteen through eighteen, is symbolic of the western quarter; and
- The seventh three layers, nineteen through twenty-one, is symbolic of the northern quarter.

"Thrice Seven," then does not simply indicate the Seven-Dimensional Universe but reveals different aspects of this Seven-Dimensional Universe incorporating its triplicate nature with respect to an aspect in some level in the divine, dynamic cosmic order (*rta*). Moreover, the combination of the Seven and Three-Dimensional Universes implicate the entire spectrum of the Vedic dharma which is *rta*, the Natural Order. Properly understood, this interpretation of "Thrice Seven" gives new meaning to the numerous passages from the Rg Veda where this phrase is found:

RV 1.72.6:

> There are three different classes of sacrifice — one in which food is being offered, two, one in which grhta is being offered; and three, in which Soma is being offered — all of which corresponds to every level of the Seven-Dimensional Universe, and the understanding of which results in the Salvation of the worshiper through the process of inner transformation brought about by the Principle of Change (Agni).

RV 1.191.12:

> The seven tongues of the Principle of Change (Agni) are multiplied in colors of red, white and black, which together eradicate and overcome Ignorance.

RV 4.1.16:

There is a Female (kine) aspect to each level and sublevel of the Seven-Dimensional Universe.

RV 7.87.4:

This rc (mantra) states that Varuna (Lord Protector of the Dynamic Cosmic Order) states that the Cow has three times seven names. Varuna (Lord Protector of the Dynamic Cosmic Order) is the divinity presiding over *rta*, the dynamics of the cosmic law. The Cow is the union of the Male (Bull) and Female (kine) Principles. The inner dynamic of the cosmos, then, runs from the operation of the Male and Female Principles.

RV 9.86.21:

From the Purified Mind (Soma) the inner secrets and knowledge of the Seven-Dimensional Universe are revealed.

RV 10.64.8:

Through the processes of inner transformation (Agni) the worshiper is made self-aware and conscious of inner secrets.

RV 10.90.15:

Purusa is impelled by the dynamic energies of the macro- and microcosmic levels of the Seven-Dimensional Universe.

The Seven-Dimension universe is the spiritual goal for the worshiper. The worshiper's ultimate goal is liberation and salvation. It is a spiritual journey. Traveling on the Vedic path to liberation and salvation, all the levels of existence in the Vedic dharma are subsumed in the Seven-Dimension universe. "Thrice Seven" is the roadmap from the material world (Two-Dimension universe) to liberation (the Seven-Dimension universe).

RV 1.164.4:

Who has seen the first-born having bones born
from that being having no bones?
I ask the Rishiis because I do not know.

A MODEST INTERPRETATION:

This rc (mantra) asks the ultimate question. How was the material sensible world ("the first-born having bones") born from the intangible, subtle principles ("the first-born having no bones") which originate from *Rta*? How was the sensible and subtle world created? The answers are to be found in the Vedas. Yet, the questions still abound.

Who is the first-born? The "first born" is the process(es) and/or principle(s) which appear out of the creation of the dynamic cosmic order (*rta*). Who or what is the "first born" of *rta*, the dynamic cosmic order?

There is no lack of usual suspects.

The Veda identifies many Vedic forces as Rta's "first born":

- Agni, the Principle of Transformation.
- The Waters. (RV 10.109.1.)
- Vayu, the manifestation of the wind. (RV 10.168.3; AV 2.1.4.)
- Brhaspati. (RV 6.73.1.)
- Prajapati. (AV 4.35.1; 12.1.6.)
- Visvakarmen. (RV 6.122.1.)
- Soma, the Principle of Divine Union and Religious Ecstacy. (RV 9.68.5.)

- The entire pantheon of dynamic Vedic forces. (RV 10.61.19.)
- A dynamic divine entity simply identified as "the first born of *rta*." (RV 10.5.7.)

That there are so many divine offspring from the Natural Order (rta) is testament both to the extraordinary breadth of its reach and its divine nature. It is fair to say that the "first born" of the dynamic cosmic order is the totality of all dynamic Vedic forces. Their qualities and powers are combined to make manifest the extreme subtlety of their forces and powers to run and regulate every aspect of the universe. After these Vedic forces are born, they operate to run the Natural Order.

"With no bones"? This is a reference no doubt to the ethereal nature of the unborn, the Eternal. The next rc (mantra) describes the encounter of mere mortals with the unborn.

RV 1.164.5:

My mind cannot conceive the principles which
pervade and rule over the Creation.

A MODEST INTERPRETATION:

This rc (mantra) is a follow-up of the previous and presents the problem to
the reader from another perspective.

This rc (mantra) recognizes the enormity of the vast cosmos presented
and the issues implicated. Humans can barely take care of their own needs,
let alone conceive or understand the inner workings of the entire Universe.
It is not simply aporia, that rational impasse, difficulty of passing, lack of
resources, or puzzlement which is the basis for all philosophical thought.
It is the awesome confrontation of the Divine, the Unspeakable, the
Unknowable.

The unknowability of the One is a sentiment is as old as the Veda itself.
(RV 1.170.1.) The belief in the ultimate divine presence as an unknowable
entity was widely shared in Upanishadic literature:

- Kena Upanishad, 1.3, states of the divine presence, "The eye does
  not go thither, nor speech, nor the mind. We do not know it; we
  do not understand how anyone can teach It. It is different from
  the known; it is above the unknown."
- Mundaka Upanishad, 3.1.8, states, "Brahman is not grasped by
  the eye, nor by speech, nor by the other senses, nor by penance or

good works. A man becomes pure through serenity of intellect; thereupon, in meditation, he beholds Him who is without parts."

- Brihadaranyaka Upanishad, 4.4.21, states, "The intelligent aspirant after Brahman, knowing about this alone, should attain intuitive knowledge. (He) should not think of too many words, for it is particularly fatiguing to the organ of speech."
- The Katha Upanishad, 2.1.11, warns, "By the mind alone is Brahman to be realized; then one does not see in It any multiplicity whatsoever."

This sense of cosmic befuddlement and wonder originated from sentiments expressed in various portions of the Rg Veda:

- RV 1.75.3 directly questions Agni, in his manifestation as the Principle of Change, asking, Who are you? Who are your kinsmen? Upon whom should we rely?
- After positing that in the very beginning there was an indiscriminate mass of matter in the universe before the solar and other cosmic systems were created, RV 10.129.6 asks, Who really knows about this?
- There was a visceral yet unattainable need to understand the universe. RV 10.88.18 wonders How many fires and suns exist? What are the numbers of dawns and waters? These questions amount to asking whether other earths and suns exists in the cosmos, a question we still ask today.

Answers to these questions are crucial to the worshiper's liberation and salvation. Knowledge of the workings of the universe equates that perfect transcendental knowledge of the infinite. (RV 1.9.1.) Knowledge and understanding of how the universe arose is the "first seed of the spirit." (RV 10.129.4.)

This rc (mantra) is structured as much as a plea in desperation as a statement of fact. How can a finite mind conceive of an infinite presence? This puts the worshiper in a dilemma. If liberation and salvation is the spiritual goal, and that goal can only be realized by knowledge of Brahman, what is a worshiper to do?

The next rc (mantra) appears to present an answer.

RV 1.164.6:

Not seeing I ask the Rishiis who see and have seen.
What holds the Creation together?
What is the One (ekam), which is the unborn?

A MODEST INTERPRETATION:

From the primeval indiscriminate mass which permeated creation, three primal forces appeared, in this order:

- *Rta*, which is luminous in the greater Vedic dharma,
- Satya, which is luminous in existence, and
- Tapas, which is the creative, internal heat of Pure Energy in Rta and Satya.

From these three essences arose the One. (RV 190; JB 3.360.) This rc (mantra) introduces the reader to Ekam, the One. The One is both an entity, a personage and an umbrella concept that includes all other concepts, forces, and energies in the Vedic dharma.

So, carrying on from the previous rc, the worshiper then poses a series of rhetorical questions about the universe to those best qualified to answer — the Rishiis to whom the mysteries of the universe are revealed.

The One, ekam, can be found in the following passages of the Rg Veda:

- In the First Mandala of the Rg Veda it is found in RV 1.31.2;
  1.93.4; 1.95.3; 1.96.5; 1.110.3, 5; 1.117.18; 1.161.2; 1.164.46;
  1.164.48; and 1.165.6.
- In the Third Mandala it is found in RV 3.1.6; 3.31.1; and 3.54.8.
- In the Fourth Mandala it is found in RV 4.16.3; 4.19.1; 4.35.2;
  4.36.4; and 4.58.4.
- In the Fifth Mandala the One is found in RV 5.32.11; 5.62.2;
  and 5.85.6.
- In the Sixth Mandala the One is found in RV 6.9.5; and 6.17.8.
- In the Seventh Mandala Ekam, the One, is found in RV 7.18.11;
  and 7.18.17.
- In the Eighth Mandala it is found in RV 8.20.13; 8.58.2; 8.100.5;
  and 8.101.6.
- In the Ninth Mandala it is found in RV 9.9.4; 9.21.3; and 9.97.55.
- In the Tenth Mandala it is found in RV 10.14.16; 10.27.16;
  10.48.7; 10.56.1; 10.80.2, 6; 10.92.15; 10.101.5; 10.109.5; 10.114.5;
  10.129.5; 10.138.6; and 10.142.6.

Some of the passages in this chart refer to the number "one." Others
pertain to the metaphysical "One." Mostly, the "One" in the Veda is
undefined. The Modest Interpretation is that the "One," Ekam, is God,
with the other Vedic deities, principles and forces being manifestations of
God. The One, Ekam, itself is mentioned with different names in the Veda:

- According to one version of creation, the One created itself from
  the primordial mass of indeterminate matter which was present at
  the beginning. (RV 10.129.2.) This is God the creator.
- Surya, the Vedic incorporating the force and principle of Energy,
  which has been translated in English translations as the "Supreme
  Being," the "Him," or "that effulgent glory of divine light," as well
  as other renderings in the Gayatri Hymn. (RV 3.62.10.)

In the Vedic Dharma, the One is that unifying principle which was
generated from the beginning stages of the Natural Order. According to
this evolution, the first to appear was the One, created by the operation of
Tapas. (RV 10.129.3.) Tapas is intense heat, concentration, or meditation.

For the purposes of the Vedic dharma, the Natural Order (*rta*), Tapas is Pure Energy, generated by the internal processes of the universe originating from the very first and indeterminate mass of undefined matter. It is communicated to humanity and appears as intense concentration or meditation. The purveyors of Tapas are the principal Vedic divine forces. The properties of Tapas, Internal Energy, are evident from the following rcs

- Agni, the Principle of Change, is the prime conveyer of the radiant heat of Internal Energy. (RV 6.5.4.)
- In an act of self-sacrifice, this radiant heat of Pure Energy is communicated to humanity when Agni burns the uncreated form of his being through the generation of Internal Energy. (RV 10.16.4.)
- The subtle personification of divine ecstasy, Soma, is the result of Internal Energy (Tapas). (RV 9.113.2.)
- On death the soul travels to Svar, the region of light, through the upward movement of Tapas. (RV 10.154.2.)
- The Seven-Dimension Universe, the transcendent world, derives its inspiration from the Internal Energy of Agni. (RV 8.60.16.)

Tapas is one of the primal energies of the Natural Order. It is the impetus of contemplative life; it is the heat of intense meditation. It is the worshiper's key for entering the transcendent Seven-Dimension World. This energy is indispensable to the salvation and liberation of the worshiper. It is an integral part of the Vedic dharma, the Natural Order (*rta*). This primordial energy is transformed and deified in the personage of Surya, which is the subject of the next rc.

RV 1.164.7:

Let him who knows declare the dynamics of Energy (Surya)
and explain how water can be evaporated by the rays of the Sun.

A MODEST INTERPRETATION:

To understand the meaning of this rc (mantra) we must first be clear about
the difference between two distinct solar Vedic forces — Surya and Savitr.

Surya is primarily an astronomical body, the Sun. Surya's energy has
the qualities of measuring the days, prolonging the days of life, driving
away sickness, disease and other evils, and the Creator of all. Ancient
commentators clarify the relationship of Surya and Savitr:

- Yaksa notes that Savitr appears when the darkness disappears.
  (Nir. 12.12.)
- Yet, commenting on RV 5.81.4, Sayana states before its rising the
  Sun is called Savitr and from the rising of dawn to its setting the
  Sun is Surya.

These two conflicting commentaries are reconciled by the Vedas in the
dynamic force inherent in Savitr. There, Savitr "approaches" or "brings"
Surya. (RV 1.35.8.) "Bringing Surya" implies a similarity but also increase.
"Bringing" anything implies a transporting agent, and in this transporting
function Savitr conveys the qualities of Surya to the worshiper and to
the other Vedic divine forces. Savitr thereby represents the Principle of
Immortality.

He bestows the benefit of immortality to other dynamic Vedic forces and to us, mere mortals:

- He also bestows immortality to the Rhbus, who were previously mortal and acquired life immortal because of his fine character. (RV 1.110.1, 2.)
- He bestows immortality to the gods and duration to humans. (RV 4.54.2.)
- After bestowing duration to the life of humans, Savitr conducts the remains of the mortal coil, the smoke of the cremated body, upwards to the heavenly World (RV 10.17.4), under the guidance and protection of Pusan (AGS 4.4.7), another Sun deity and member of the Adityas (astrological houses).

Savitr is also the Principle of Creation:

- This principle is the ultimate giver of life. (RV 1.22.7.)
- This principle is responsible for all physical manifestation. (RV 6.71.2.)
- Savitr fosters the lives of successive generations. (RV 4.54.2.)
- The Principle of Creation establishes the fullness of being. (RV 7.45.11.)
- With these attributes this principle creates the entire work of creation. (RV 2.38.1, 2.)

There are two sides of the divine force of Savitr. These aspects are complimentary. The work of creation itself is a perpetual process: the soul, as the world, is eternal. (RV 2.38.1.) Those powers are harmonized in a sacrificial context by the Golden Man, Purusa. (SPB 7.4.1.25, 32, 43; 7.4.3.1, 14, 17, 19; 7.5.2.11; 8.1.4.11; 10.5.2.6, 7, 8; 10.5.4.14, 15.) Thus, there are two powers at work. On a physical level Surya implicates the process of evaporation, and the other Savitr is the continual power inherent in that natural process. One level of interpretation of 1.164.7 invokes Surya and is scientific, asking those who understand the physics of water evaporation to explain those dynamics. On a deeper mystical level Savitr is invoked and is a commentary of the principle of regeneration.

The rain originates from water evaporated by the Sun; once deposited in the clouds, the water droplets return to the earth as rain, only to return to the clouds to fall again as rain. It is an eco-system taught in high school science classes, but also emblematic of the regeneration and rejuvenation of the natural system.

If one had to contrast Savitr and Surya, one could say that while both are dynamic Vedic forces, Surya is a degree or two below Savitr. The golden element of Savitr augments this interpretation. Surya's characteristic as the Principle of Energy gives this dynamic an added dimension. When the Rishii is requesting those who "knows the dynamics of Energy," with the interposition of Savitr as the Principle of Immortality, the Rishii appears to articulate his version of the scientific principle of the Conservation of Energy, that energy itself never dissipates or is lost but merely changes into a different form.

There is a deeper meaning at work. On an occult and symbolic level and as an ultimate paradox, Fire and Water contain the same essential nature and origin. The essential equivalence of fire and water is reflected in the elements found in the sacrifice, in the sacrificial grass:

- The sacrificial grass is the cosmic, primeval, Water. (Gonda, *The Ritual Functions and Significance of Grasses in the Religion of the Veda*, (1985), p. 36.)
- Agni as Fire is produced out of the water from which the grass is represented. (SPB 2.2.3.1; 1.2.3.9; BSS 5.19.8.)
- This is how Change (Agni) is kindled (idhyase) in the waters. (RV 3.25.5.)
- In its many regenerative properties, the bull representing the symbol of the creative, generative power in the universe, Agni and the Maruts, whose active principles are several, are responsible for arkam, which is interpreted by Sayana as the descending waters and is the luminous nature of Indra. (RV 1.19.4.)
- The sacrificial Agni (fires) are established in the rainy season.

Agni, the principle of Change and Transformation, supplies the active principles conjoining the qualities of combustibility and fluidity found in Fire and Water. This is the mystery of the natural cosmic order that the Rishii appears to convey: That the cosmic order is a symbiotic vortex of reconciled opposites, one complementing the other. This mystery is reflected in simple physical processes, to the minutest workings of the cosmos, to the broadest expanse of the divine, dynamic cosmic order (*rta*).

RV 1.164.8:

The mother (earth) worships the father (Sun) that she may receive water.
The earth receives this water by "impregnation."
He anticipates her needs with his mind and
communicates one to the other.

A MODEST INTERPRETATION:

This rc (mantra) is highly metaphorical and explains the relationship between the Sun and the earth. The Rishi Dirghatama understood that without the warmth of the Sun life on earth would not exist. The Rishi Dirghatama explained this relationship by describing the relationship in religious terms.

Yet the rc (mantra) speaks in scientific, physical terms. Properly understood with reference to the previous rc. RV 1.164.7, it explains the visible phenomenon of water evaporating in the Sun. This rc (mantra) explains that the evaporated water rises to the clouds and "impregnates" the earth only to return as rain.

Evaporation is a simple process. But how does the Sun evaporate the water? The innovation in this rc (mantra) is the explanation of the Sun's ability to evaporate water. The rc (mantra) states that the Sun anticipates the earth's need [for water] with his Mind. While Rishi Dirghatama, the author to whom the Asyavamasya Sukta was revealed, likely did not understand the mechanics of nuclear fission, he understood that the brightness of the Sun was due to internal processes within the Sun itself, creating the heat which emanates outward. These internal processes are the Sun's "mind," and the rays reflect the fluctuations (vrttis) of the Sun's "mind."

This process is the "communication" exchanged between the earth and the Sun. This communication establishes and comprises the cosmic order (*rta*). The communication also reflects the flip-side of *Rta* as representative of the sacrifice and sacrificial rite. This rite consists of the exchange between the immanent and the transcendent. Therefore, just as the earth communicates with the Sun, the worshiper communicates with the divine through the sacrificial rite.

RV 1.164.9:

The mother (Earth) is yoked on the right side of the axle.
Its womb is rested in the clouds.
The calf (rain) bellows in three places.
It looks to its mother which manifests in three spaces.

A MODEST INTERPRETATION:

"The mother (Earth) is yoked on the right side of the axle."

The rc (mantra) states that the earth is yoked on the right side of the axle. In the Vedic world, just as in politics, there is a distinction between left and right-side matter. To fully understand this distinction in a Vedic context, we need to backtrack a bit.

Officially, saman is a type of Vedic chanting. This type of chanting is reserved especially for the Soma sacrifice, and in one Veda in particular, the SamaVeda. This Veda, while concerning Soma, the plant, the deity, the source of divine inspiration, is so named because the samans are to be used during the Soma Sacrifice as the Sama chant. There are two aspects to Saman.

- The material meaning of the word is associated with the practice of yajna.
- The esoteric meaning of saman, developed more fully in later Vedas, is "vital force" a forerunner to "prana," and the cause of creation itself. On a deeper level the esoteric meaning of saman is

a correspondence of the expanding and contracting movements of the universe, on the micro- and macrocosmic levels. (BU 6.6.20.)

On a deep, esoteric level *rta*, the sacrifice, is the representation of the universe, with its own movement and sequence of events. *Rta*, the dynamic energy of the Vedic dharma, is sacrifice. *Rta* is also the saman, the hymns and chanting recited during the sacrifice. (RV 1.147.1.) There is a mutual equivalence between *rta*, which is sacrifice, yagna, and saman. (RV 8.25.4.) That equivalence originates from the presence of motion and movement in the cosmos.

Saman is the melody sung in verses (rcs) at the yagna (sacrifices) and is modified as any melody is by highs, lows, insertions, lengthenings, intonations — any components which make a song. Sama is the melodies sung at the sacrifice (yagna) but these chanting travels through the atmosphere with sound waves, a fact the Rishis must certainly have understood, because of the mystic significance they attributed to the chant which will be discussed a little later. But first, the preliminary principles which serve as the foundation allowing Saman to represent the movement of the universe.

Vibration is the subtle aspect of energy. This energy permeates the Natural Order (*rta*). On a sub-atomic level is reflected in the movement of atoms, and it is present in the saman, chanting, in the sacrifice. Divine Duality (the Asvins) assists the power and energy of Divine grace and Knowledge (Indra) to give rise to the Right and Left-Handed movements of the universe, from which sama is the sacrificial representation. For this reason, Sama is responsible for making all objects in the universe visible. (TB 2.2.8.7.) The movements of sama undulate with the outward and inward breathes of prana while the hymns are chanted or otherwise; sama also travels inward and outward, rhythmically, as the chanter performs the sama song or mantra.

The physical manifestation of these expansion/contraction movements are reflected in the physical effects of the sound vibrations of musical notes traveling through the air. In the same way, the upward and downward aspirations of the Sama chant affect the vibration of the air around and about the chanter. We saw how these upward and downward aspirations affected both the inner prana of the chanter and the air around him. In this way, the Sama chant creates the environment for both the microcosm, represented by the Saman Chanter, and the macrocosm, the air around the chanter and beyond. On a deeper level, recalling that there is a five-fold sama chant, representing the subtle aspect of the microcosmic material world of the Five-Dimension Universe, and a seven-fold sama chant, representing the transcendent world of the Seven-Dimension Universe. This is the ultimate esoteric meaning of sama: the rhythms of expansion and contraction permeating in *rta*, the Natural Order.

In the execution of Vedic chanting, vibration serve an important function in the Natural Order. The interplay between the left and right movements of sama is esoteric, and has an occult meaning which is unknown to most. (RV 2.27.11.) The esoteric meaning of sama is that it represents the expanding and contracting vibrations of the dynamic energies of the universe, through the powers of Conjunction and Unity (Indra). The sequential aspects of *Rta* establishes the vibration in the cosmos which regulate the motion and movement of all things. The sequential aspects of sama translates that vibration from the rhythms and cadences of the hymns at the sacrifice. These two sequential aspects are reflected in the oscillations between the left and right-handed movements. In this way the expansion/contraction movements of sama represent the left and right-hand movements of the cosmic order.

The duality of those movements also finds their place in the Two-Dimensional Universe. Just a few of the dual movements present in this universe are found in the following chart:

Right-Handed Movement	Left-Handed Movement
Sun	Moon
CounterClockwise	Clockwise
West	East
South	North
Hot	Cold
Fire	Earth
Creation	Dissolution
Regeneration	Creation
Expansion	*Contraction*

The left and right-handed motions of the universe are a reflection in the Vedic divinities, in particular, with Indra. The contracting, uniting, and conjoining powers of Indra are quite extensive and include the following:

- protect the worshiper with all the powers of purification (Soma). (RV 8.4.8.)
- bestowing spiritual riches to the worshiper after receiving the same. (RV 5.36.4.)
- by protecting all humans from the perils of evil. (RV 8.24.6.)
- by bringing spiritual blessings to the worshiper. (RV 8.81.6.)

The right and left movements are related to the mental states a worshiper seeks to emulate.

- The right-handed movement of discernment is reflected in and a product of the sacrifice itself, which establishes consciousness, mind and thought. (VYV 4.19; 4.23; TS 1.2.5.6 - 8.)
- The left-handed movement of the blessing is based on the action of giving. (RV 1.4.22; TS 1.4.22; VYS 8.2.)

The material and esoteric are then harmonized in the Saman chant. Saman is the Word (Vak). In this sense the Word is the articulation of the material universe. This Word is represented by the divine sound, nada, and is established at the beginning of the universe's creation. With articulation the indiscriminate mass which existed before the beginning is given form. The evolution from the divine sound to creation is represented by Om, the divine sound, to Saman, the articulation and manifestation of form, the Word.

On a physical level the vibration in the universe is made in the articulation of the original sacred syllable, OM. At the very creation of each kalpa, the cycle beginning the appearance of the universe, the sacred syllable makes its appearance. At that moment, the Divine Sound, OM, resonates, and from that sound the Vedas, specifically, the Rg Veda, among all other things, are articulated. At that point, the operational mechanism of Sama is born. Sama is the vocal reflection of nada, articulated in the chant recited at the sacrifice, and represents the divine vibration of the universe after its creation and is reflected in all the aspects of that creation. Sama, then, is not just the chant at the sacrifice. This is its external reflection. Internally, esoterically, it represents the very vibration of the universe in its macrocosmic and microcosmic aspects.

That the earth is yoked on the right side of the axle is consistent with the Satapatha Brahmana, 1.2.5.6 - 8, which indicates that this material world is the product of discernment, reflected in and a product of the sacrifice itself, and established in consciousness, mind and thought.

"Its womb is rested in the clouds.
The calf (rain) bellows in three places.
It looks to its mother which manifests in three spaces."

The calf bellows in "three places," and the calf's mother appears in those "three places." This is a reference to the Three-Dimensional Universe which is the subtle representation of the material world. The Veda interprets the mother as heaven and her calf as the earth. (RV 1.32.9; 8.88.6; 10.119.4.) Other comparisons state the mother cow as the sacrificial hymn and the calf as Indra, the Vedic force of divine grace. (RV 3.61.5; 9.61.14; 9.86.2.) There are other implications about Bovine knowledge which are explained in detail in RV 1.164.26. Here, however, the rc (mantra) equates the calf as rain. Rain in the coded language of the Veda is symbolic of the principle of regeneration, is associated with the Vedic dynamism in Indra, and consists of water. This water is sourced from rain that accumulates in the clouds, in the abode of Indra (RV 1.7.6), where Indra is the rainmaker. (RV 4.26.2; 5.35.5; 10.23.4; 10.43.7.) According to this rc (mantra) that rainmaker is also the calf. The functional equivalence of the Calf and Indra is thereby established.

This rc (mantra) presents a fundamental feature of the Vedic dharma (*rta*): The cosmic order constantly renews and regenerates itself. The energy of the universe is never dissipated or destroyed but changes form or substance. Amid all the fluctuations there is one constant. That entity, the One, is introduced in the next rc (mantra).

RV 1.164.10:

The One living in the skies has three mothers and three fathers.
These parents speak in a voice that comprehends all but does not move.

A MODEST INTERPRETATION:

Continuing from the previous rc, one passage from the Rg Veda mentions
that the Calf has two mothers. (RV 3.33.3.) This rc (mantra) raises the bar
and speaks of three mothers and three fathers.

The Vedic dharma (*rta*) understands ("a voice that comprehends"),
informs, pervades and regulates this material world we all live in, the
Three-Dimensional Universe. This rc (mantra) analyzes the constituent
parts of the Seven-Dimensional Universe. This meaning is found from the
elements found in the rc (mantra) — The One + three mothers + three
fathers. These elements comprise, part and parcel, the Seven Dimension
Universe, and, by implication, *rta*, the Vedic dharma. The Vedic dharma
is immutable, and it does not change ("does not move"). *Rta*, the Natural
Order, pervades the higher wisdom that the worshiper seeks to understand
and to experience and incorporate.

RV 1.164.11:

Formed with twelve spokes, by length of time, unweakened,
this wheel of the Natural Order (*rta*) rolls around heaven.
Agni stands joined in pairs together, seven hundred and twenty sons.

A MODEST INTERPRETATION:

This rc (mantra) points to two separate expanses of time, one for the earth, reflected in the twelve months to the year, and the other for the great cosmos beyond the earth, reflected in the twelve houses of the zodiac ("seven hundred and twenty sons"). The Natural Order, the Vedic dharma (*rta*), establishes the asterisms and houses in the zodiac. RV 1.164.11 implicates the asterisms in the zodiac itself ("Formed with twelve spokes"), describing its progression across the sky. It is the cosmic order (*rta*) which creates the three-dimensional world ("three naves"). The principle of Change (Agni) conveys the influence of the asterisms and zodiac to the level of the sensible world. In so conveying the Principle of Change (Agni) informs the sensible world of the higher wisdom contained in the macrocosm.

"Twelve Spokes"

There are two interpretations of the Twelve Spokes. On one level the spokes refer to the zodiac. On another, these spokes refer to the months of the Year. Both interpretations are mutually harmonious, as the former urges and gives birth to the latter. Both are integral elements to Vedic dharma, the Natural Order (*rta*). That the Twelve Spokes refer to the months of the year is not a likely interpretation, however, because the Vedic annual calendar was not standardized; some versions have seven months and other versions four.

The most likely interpretation is the Vedic zodiac. This rc (mantra) is all about the zodiac, and the zodiac is all about the Adityas. The Satapatha Brahmana describes how the Adityas began. That beginning was somewhat haphazard. In the beginning the dynamic cosmic order (*rta*) established the following classification of dynamic Vedic energies:

- Eight Vasus. (SPB, 4.5.7.2.)
- Eleven Rudras. (SPB, 4.5.7.2.)
- Twelve Adityas. (SPB, 4.5.7.2.)
- Heaven and Earth, making the thirty-second and thirty-third deities. (SPB, 4.5.7.2.)
- Prajapati, consisting of the thirty-fourth dynamic Vedic energy. (SPB, 4.5.7.2.)

When Prajapati created the world, he united his mind with Speech (vak). The result of this union was that he became pregnant with and created eight, eleven and twelve drops:

- The eight drops were the Vasus. (SPB, 4.5.7.2; 6.1.2.6, 10.)
- The eleven drops were the Rudras. (SPB, 4.5.7.2; 6.1.2.6, 10.)
- The twelve drops were the Adityas. (SPB, 4.5.7.2; 6.1.2.6, 10.)

Prajapati thereupon placed these deities in various sectors of the universe:

- The Vasus were placed on earth. (SPB, 6.1.2.6, 10.)
- The Rudras were placed in the air. (SPB, 6.1.2.6, 10.)
- The Adityas were placed in the sky. (SPB, 6.1.2.6, 10.)

The Adityas are the offspring of Aditi. Aditi herself is the representation of the highest infinitude. According to the Veda (RV 1.89.10), Aditi consists of the following:

- Heaven and Earth;
- Father and Son;
- The collective energies of the dynamic Vedic energies;
- All that was, all that is, and all that will be; and
- The expanse of the Five-Dimensioned Universe.

The Rg Veda (RV 2.27.11; 10.72.9) and Satapatha Brahmana (SPB 1.3.1.2, 3) establish eight Adityas (Astrological Houses):

- Mitra;
- Aryama;
- Bhaga;
- Varuna;
- Daksa;
- Amsha;
- Martanda.

Martanda was "cast off" by Aditi. (RV 10.72.8.) Martunda reappeared in the Tattiriya Aranyaka when it reincarnated as Visvasvan with Indra. (T.A., 1.13.3.) This still leaves nine Adityas. Elsewhere, the Satapatha Brahmana (Wikipedia, article on the Adityas at *http://en.wikipedia.org/wiki/%C4%80dityas#cite_note-3*) establishes twelve Adityas (Astrological Houses) with the following members:

- Mitra.
- Aryama.
- Bhaga.
- Varuna.
- Daksa.
- Indra.
- Amsha.
- Savitr.
- Yama.
- Ravi.
- Dhatr.
- Surya.

This is how the astrological houses should be considered. There are the twelve Adityas, and they represent the twelve Houses of the Zodiac. (Murthy, *Vedic View of the Earth* (1997).) The Adityas preside over the astrological houses. The next chart contains the twelve houses of the zodiac, Western counterparts, and, with slight variations, the presiding deity:

Western Zodiac Sign	Vedic Zodiac Sign	Presiding Vedic Energies (Adityas)
Aries	Mesa	Aryama
Taurus	Vrsabha	Mitra
Gemini	Mithuna	Varuna
Cancer	Karkata	Indra
Leo	Simha	Visvasvan
Virgo	Kanya	Pusan (Savitr)
Libra	Tula	Parjanja
Scorpius	Vrscika	Asmshu
Saggitarius	Dhanus	Bhaga
Capricorn	Makara	Tvastha
Aquarius	Kumba	Visnu
Pisces	Mina	Dhata

There is a symbiotic relationship between the dynamic cosmic order, *rta*, and the zodiacal houses. *Rta*, the Natural Order, created the astrological houses in the Adityas. The expansiveness of Aditi is reflected on her offspring, the Adityas. At the same time, the astrological houses are symbolized by the Adityas, who

- commandeer *rta*, the Vedic dharma. (RV 3.2.8; 4.10.2; 6.55.1; 7.66.12; 8.83.3.)
- are the Guardians of the Vedic dharma. (RV 1.1.8; 5.10.2; 5.63.1; 6.49.15; 6.51.3; 9.48.1; 9.73.1; 10.8.5.)

The Veda states the Adityas — and their corresponding astrological houses — encompass

- Heaven.

- Earth.
- The mid-world.
- Father and son.
- The Adityas (astrological houses) are all that was, is and will be. (RV 1.89.10.)

Indeed, the worshiper is a composite of the astrological houses:

Vedic Zodiac Sign (macrocosm)	The Worshiper (microcosm)
Mesa (Aryama)	Head
Vrsabha (Mitra)	Face
Mithuna (Varuna)	Arms
Karkata (Indra)	Heart
Simha (Visvasvan)	Stomach
Kanya (Pusan)	Hip
Tula (Parjanja)	Space Below Navel
Vrscika (Asmshu)	Genitals
Dhanus (Bhaga)	Thighs
Makara (Tvastha)	Knees
Kumba (Visnu)	Ankles
Mina (Dhata)	Feet

In the Vedic path to salvation and liberation the worshiper may seek spiritual and personal guidance from the astrological houses. This occult area is perhaps the least understood and most obscure portion of the Veda. Much of its substance is forever lost due to the great antiquity of the Veda. Therefore, the art of modernly astrology has been considerably diminished, is frequently subject to corruption, quackery, and trivialization, and one may easily to be overly obsessed by the prognostication of future events as purportedly foretold by the stars. The real issue the Vedas address is whether and to what extent this astral wisdom may assist the worshiper in the journey for Vedic salvation. Yet, somewhere, that wisdom may be obtained.

The general stellar population — the planets, stars, and the constellations, and the ecliptic relations of the planets, stars, and the constellations — each play their role to influence the worshiper's salvation. This stellar population is the "wheel of order (*rta*)" regulating the universe, the individuals who live under that universe, and the worshiper seeing to re-unite with that universe.

The Adityas, as is the worshiper, are subordinate to and are subject to the dictates of *rta*, the natural, cosmic order, and the worshiper should incorporate the following dictates in the Vedic path to liberation and salvation:

- The Adityas (the astrological houses) are faithful to the laws of the divine cosmic order (*rta*). (RV 4.24.4; 8.59.4.)
- The Adityas (the astrological houses) are dependent on the laws of the divine cosmic order (*rta*). (RV 1.113.12; 5.61.14; 6.3.1.)
- The laws of *rta*, the divine cosmic order, are responsible for the placement and maintenance of the astrological houses (Adityas) and the moon (Soma). (RV 2.27.8; 10.85.1.)

The Adityas, the asterisms and their houses, also give birth the Year. The twelve months of the year are established with reference to twelve houses of the zodiac. From the twelve Adityas (astrological houses) arise the twelve months. While opinions vary as to the precise number, there were twelve months to the Rg Vedic year. (Warandpante, *New Light on the Date of the Rg Veda* (1994), p. 24.) The Adityas (the astrological houses) correspond to the twelve months of the year (RV 7.103.9; TS 5.4.12; AB 1.30; TB 3.8.10; KB 11.6; PB 6.2.2; SPB 1.3.5.11; SPB, 11.6.3.8), as set in the following chart:

The astrological houses (Adityas) give birth to the year. The year in Vedic thought signifies more than a measurement of time. The year is that which defines the substance of absolute time experienced on a material level, as opposed to that region beyond time and space. (TS 6.5.3.1.) This "year" is the twelve referenced in this rc. Thus, the year is responsible for the cyclical movement of the seasons and the immutable and orderly succession of the Natural Order. In addition, the year is the process of evolution and dissolution, as in that passage which states that the year causes some things to perish and other things to come into existence. (AA, 3.2.3; SPB 10.4.3.1.) The "twelve" in this rc (mantra) therefore has a double meaning, one for the Adityas, the zodiacal houses and the other signifying the year, the creation of the zodiacal houses.

"The Wheel Rolls Around"

In keeping with the regular succession of seasons and years the year has been likened to a wheel, not only in this rc (mantra) but in other passages:

- The year is the revolving wheel of god. (KB 20.1.1.)
- The month has thirty spokes and the year has twelve spokes. (AV 4.35.4.)

"Agni Stands Joined in Pairs Together"

Agni, in his manifestation of the Principle of Change reconciles opposites. For instance, it reconciles the powers of the Sun and the Moon:

- The Principle of Change (Agni) is identified with the Sun, Surgher, Savitr. (RV 1.57.1; 4.11.1; 3.11.1; 4.13.1.)
- On an astronomical level, the Principle of Change (Agni) moves the celestial sphere where the sky is fixed, and with the help of the Rishis (stars) leads this sphere like a horse. (RV 3.2.7.)
- The Principle of Change (Agni) holds the rim of the celestial sphere that holds the sun. (RV 2.5.1.)
- At the same time, the Principle of Change (Agni) is identified with the moon. (RV 1.27.6, 12; 5.101.4; 4.2.19; 5.6.5; 1.27.11; 3.25.3; 5.81; 1.6.5, 6; 5.11.1.)

Read together, these rcs hold that the Principle of Change (Agni) unites the dynamics of the Sun and the Moon.

Agni, in addition is the Sacrificial Fire, and is the spiritual go-between these and other Vedic forces and energies, including Heaven and the worshiper, symbolically called "Earth." (RV 7.2.3.) At that point, Agni as the Mystic Fire presides over and unites Heaven and the center of the Earth. (RV 1.59.2.) The Mystic Fire carries the powers of unification, and the Mystic Fire unites by the heat of forced fusion of opposites. The fusion occurs when Agni as the Mystic Fire enters into the worshiper and other Vedic energies and forces. (RV 7.49.4.) Just as the Sacrificial Fire is kindled by the heat produced by the rubbing of two sticks, whenever two polar opposites are united, heat is produced. This is the basis of the Mystic

Fire. On a macrocosmic level, the Mystic Fire as the Messenger is indeed a fearsome force. RV 4.7.11 describes the Mystic Messenger as "swift," roaring in the wind, consuming all and everything with its blazing fire. The convergence of these Vedic energies is indeed mystic. It is the result of a mystical fire. The results of this fusion of forces yields tangible results. On a microcosmic level, this mystic convergences produce the following treasures to be discovered and utilized by the worshiper during the spiritual journey:

"Seven Hundred and Twenty Sons"

Deciphering this passage does not require mystical or metaphysical interpretation, but simple mathematics. There are 360 days to a year. The 720 sons refer to two years.

RV 1.164.12:

The father has five feet and twelve forms in
the farthest end of the hemisphere.
The father consists of water.
He is placed on a chariot having seven wheels.

A MODEST INTERPRETATION:

The cosmic, natural, order (*rta*) establishes the sacrificial rite. The Five-Dimension Universe is associated with the sacrificial rite because the altar is constructed in five layers, representing these dimensions. The twelve forms refer to the calendar year, from which the sacrificial rites are held, and the zodiacal houses which influence human behavior. The water refers to that which is sprinkled during the sacrificial rite. The seven-wheeled chariot refers to the Seven-Dimensional Universe, the salvation and liberation found in it which is the goal of the worshiper's travels.

"The Father Has Five Feet ..."

The significance of the cardinal number five is explained in the following rc, RV 1.164.13. The Five-Dimensional Universe is the subtle aspect of the material world, the gateway to the transcendent Seven-Dimensional Universe.

"... and Twelve Forms"

The "twelve forms" is another reference to the Adityas. The number twelve has astronomical and astrological connotations, and in that capacity, is represented by the Adityas, the zodiacal houses. The Adityas (astrological houses) have far-reaching implications to the Vedic dharma (*rta*) and its constituent parts:

- The Adityas (astrological houses) give birth to the twelve incarnations of divine ecstacy and union (Soma), based on the meters found in the sama chant. (RV 10.114.5.) This is taken to mean that there are twelve forms of divine ecstasy, each offering its own spiritual blessing. It is with these incarnations the worshiper seeks to emulate and receive and channel the energy of the Natural Order (*rta*).
- The Adityas (astrological houses) provide the foundation for the twelve daksinas. (SPB 5.5.5.9.) Daksina is discrimination. (RV 1.95.6.) Daksina is the southern path undertaken by the soul after death (RV 10.17.9; 2.27.11) but is also the right-handed path (RV 10.17.9), signifying the holistic entirety of the Natural Order (*rta*).

"The Father Consists of Water"

Water has incredibly rich and diverse range of meaning in and application to the Natural Order. On a purely ritualistic level, Sindhu S. Dange has outlined at least seventeen different ritualistic meanings of water. (See, Dange, *Vedic Beliefs and Practices*, (2005), pp. 120, et seq.) As per the Seven Eternal Laws of the Veda, Water is representative for:

- The Eternal Law of Consciousness, water is emblematic to describe the mental flow of consciousness, translated in the symbols of rivers and floods.
- The Eternal Law of Sacrifice, it is representative of the sanctification of life.
- The Eternal Law of Salvation, it represents the purification of the soul.

More importantly, the Waters, are symbolic and representative of what is known in Hinduism as "the Field." The Field gained currency much later in the Bhavagad Gita, when Krishna taught Arjuna the difference between "the Field" and the "Knower of the Field." (BG, 13.) The Field was generally described as the body of Krishna, but a closer examination reveals that the Field is none other than the microcosmic Vedic dharma, the sum total of those elements which comprise the sentient consciousness. Apart from the innumerable references of the Waters in the Rg Veda, subsequent Vedic scripture indicates that the Waters represent the currents or fields which permeate the Natural Order. Thus, the Waters, and its modifications, represent

- Apah, the field or current of consciousness. (TA, 1.1.1.)
- Apam, the field or current of pervasive energy. (TA, 1.1.1.)
- Somapaam, the field or current of the living essence of physical matter. (RV 3.41.5; 8.17.3; 8.92.8.)
- Pavamana, the unmanifested field or current of physical matter.
- Madhu, the field or current of higher consciousness.

These and other fields carry with them their own specific characteristics, but all fill and pervade the Natural Order and share the nature of possessing a living life force. The Rishiis spoke in symbols and gave these processes the most recognizable name available which would still describe their function. These processes consequently were collectively called "the Waters." Krishna later in the Bhavagad Gita placed all these processes into one category — the Field.

This incredible range of meaning owes to the early realization that without water life on earth would be impossible. And this is because even before the universe came into creation, Water, an undifferentiated fluid called Sallila, pervaded everywhere and everything. (RV 10.129.3.) It is for this reason that this rc (mantra) calls water the "father," literally the generating agent containing the seed from which life is born. This concept was carried forward in the Brahmanas, where it was said that Vak, Speech, created the Waters. (SPB 6.1.1.9.) The Asyavamasya Sukta will have more to say about Vak in the later rcs.

"He Is Placed On A Chariot Having Seven Wheels"

This reference to the Seven-Dimensional Universe explained in detail in RV 1.164.12. "Chariot" has other meanings in the Rg Veda:

- In the Katha Upanishad, the body.
- The asterisms.
- The path undertaken by the astronomical or astrological bodies.

- The path undertaken by the worshiper in the journey to salvation and liberation.

In the next rc (mantra) there is a change in focus, in which the Rishii continues with his explanation of cosmology in the Vedic dharma.

The Sukta continues with this cosmology in the next rc (mantra).

RV 1.164.13

All beings reside in a five-spoked revolving wheel that is not heated.
The Five Agents rule in alternative order,
Each overtaking the other in order to live.

Cantong qi: 2.63: 1 - 2.
The Seal of the Unity of Three,
Pregadio, trans.

A MODEST INTERPRETATION:

Now is the time to discuss the next level of reality, the Five-Dimensional
Universe. There are two aspects to the Five-Dimensional Universe. One
aspect is the macrocosm. All beings reside in the Five-Dimensional
Universe. The other aspect is the macrocosm. In this rc (mantra) the Rishi
Dirghatama shifts focus on the wheel to the second aspect, the microcosm.
It is not only representative of the Five-Dimensional Universe, but the
"rolling" aspect implicates the fluctuations (vrttis) of the mind. It thereby
becomes symbolic of consciousness. This rc (mantra) then pictures the
macrocosm and microcosm in the Five-Dimensional Universe.

The double nature of this level of existence is summarized in a Shaivite
tantra, the Vijnana Bhairava Tantra. One of the visualizations the worshiper
is to use in the path to liberation is to meditate on the five voids. The five
voids consist of the five subtle tanmatras, which eventually give rise to the
five gross senses of touch, taste, sight, hearing and smell. (VBT, 32.)

The Five-Dimensional Universe is the first level of transcendence beyond the material world. Various Vedic and Hindu texts refer to the Five-Dimensional Universe. Sri Suresvara, the contemporary of Adi Sankara, notes that from a material viewpoint there are five elements to this dimension because that universe consists of fire, water, air, earth and akasha (space). (TOBV, 1.128.) While these are physical constituents, they remain nonetheless the subtle aspects of fire, water, air, earth and akasha (space). This Five-Dimensional Universe is described in the Vasistha Samhita, a Hatha Yoga text from the Eleventh Century grounded in the Vedas. According to the Vasistha Samhita (VS, 5.8), the Five-Dimensional Universe consists of:

- Bhokta, the enjoyer.
- Bhogya, the object of enjoyment.
- Bhukti, the enjoyment obtained.
- Bhogayatana, the body.
- Indriya, the sense organs.

These elements are reflected in an ontological level. The Rg Veda contemplates five types of being (RV 1.7.9; 2.2.10; 6.11.4; 9.101.9), with the material correlate, as consisting of:

- inert matter (bhur);
- prana (bhuvah);
- mind (manah);
- supermind (mahas); and
- bliss (jana or maya).

These levels of being are translated into a Five-Dimensional Universe, each level having a psychic correlate and belonging to the following astrological house or astronomical world:

- Bhuh, consisting of Bhumi, representing Growth;
- Bhuvah, consisting of Candra, representing decay, and Prthvi, representing Change (Agni);
- Svah, consisting of Surya and Rodasi representing the First Birth;

- Janah, consisting of Paramesthi, and Mahah, consisting of Krandasi, representing the First Existence; and
- Satyam, consisting of Svyambha, and Tapah, consisting of Samyati, representing Pure Being.

While the worshiper travels along the Vedic path to liberation and salvation, the Five-Dimensional Universe, as the other possible universes, represent the inner progression of the worshiper's mental and spiritual state as well as the outer world surrounding the worshiper. This is the schematic representation of the Five-Dimensional Universe:

Macrocosmic Level	Microcosmic Level	Level of Being	Psychic Correlate	Astrological House	Astronomical Entity
Bhuh	Bhur	Matter	Growth	Vrushabh (Taurus)	Bhumi (Earth)
Bhuvah	Bhuvah	Prana	Decay, Change	Kanya (Virgo)	Prthvi (World) Candra (Moon)
Svah	Manah	Mind	First Birth	Kumbh (Aquarius)	Surya (Sun) Rodasi (Heaven and Earth)
Janah Mahah	Mahas	Supermind	First Existence	Mithun (Gemini)	Krandasi (Heaven and Earth) Paramesthi (Beyond Heaven)
Satyam Tapas	Jana Maya	Bliss	Pure Being		Samyati

Special attention should be given to the last column featuring the corresponding astronomical phenomena. The Five Stages of Being each correspond to an astronomical object:

- Bhumi (RV 1.52.12; 1.64.5; 1.164.51; 2.30.9; 4.26.2; 4.57.8; 5.59.4; 5.84.1; 5.85.4; 6.67.6; 8.14.5; 10.18.10; 10.27.13; 10.58.3;

10.59.3; 10.90.1; 10.90.5; 10.14.2) is material manifestation of the planet, the earth element.

- Prthvi is the world and its surrounding atmosphere.
- Candra is the moon. (SPB 4.12.25.)
- Surya is the sun.
- Rodasi (RV 1.52.10; 1.105.1 - 18; 1.167.4 5; 1.185.3; 3.26.9; 3.54.3, 4, 10; 4.55.6; 4.56.4, 8; 6.50.5; 6.62.8; 6.66.6; 6.70.2, 3; 9.7.9; 9.98.9; 10.12.4; 10.67.11; 10.79.4; 10.88.5, 10; 10.92.11) is the first manifestation of heaven and earth when they are conjoined.
- Krandasi (RV 2.12.8; 6.25.4; 10.121.6) is the second manifestation of heaven and earth conjoined.
- Paramesthi is that spatial area beyond heaven and earth. It is that spatial region wherein resides the highest personage in the universe. (SPB 3.10.9.) Later traditions indicate that paramesthi is the region where Brahma (SPB 3.13.6), the creator of the universe (SPB 2.8.25) resides.
- Samyati (RV 2.12.8; 5.37.5; 9.68.3; 9.69.3), that place of Pure Being, is beyond the spatial and temporal expanses of heaven and earth.

This scheme is summarized in this chart:

Stage of Being	Astronomical Object
Bhumi	World
Prthvi	Earth
Candra	Moon
Surya	Sun
Rodasi	Heaven and Earth
Krandasi	Heaven and Earth
Paramesthi	Beyond Heaven
Samyati	

This chart is an astronomical representation of the ever-elevated stages of existence, from Bhumi, the world, to the highest stage, above and beyond heaven. The individual psyche, the worshiper, travels upwards through these stages until achieving final liberation at Samyati.

The Five-Dimensional Universe is the gateway to the Seven-Dimensional Universe. The Purified Mind (Soma) governs the five cardinal points of the universe. (RV 9.86.29.) These cardinal points correspond to the Five-Dimensional Universe. Here in the Five-Dimensional Universe, is where spiritual development of the worshiper begins to identify with the higher regions of the universe. Eventually, the worshiper progresses beyond the reaches of space and time, the region of divine ecstacy and bliss which is personified by Purification (Soma).

A presiding divinity governs each level. Those presiding divinities are:

Bhuh:	The Principle of Change (Agni)
Candra:	Purification (Soma)
Surya:	The Principle of Change (Agni)
Parameshthi:	Purification (Soma)
Svyambhu:	The Principle of Change (Agni)

The Five-Dimensional Universe has a sacrificial element. It represents the Sacrificial Altar, which the Brahmanas describe as consisting of five layers. (SPB 6.1.2.18; 6.2.3.10; 10.1.5.3.) "Citi," is defined by Monier Williams as both "layer" or "stratum" as well as "knowledge" or "consciousness." It is for this reason that it is said that the Sacrificial Altar, particularly the Fire-Altar (Agnistoma) represents the light or consciousness and Knowledge. (SPB 6.6.6.17; 10.2.6.15; 10.3.2.13; 10.4.3.10; 19.5.3.12.) The Five-Dimensional Universe describes the five stages of purification described in RV 1.140.2:

- Polar opposites are united.
- The internal dynamics of spiritual clarity (grhta) and inner purity (Soma).
- Mental and Spiritual regeneration, the product of the internal dynamics.

- Mental and Spiritual strength.
- The worshiper is born again, twice-born, casting away the previous self.

The Five-Dimensional world corresponds to the material world, and multiples of Five are reflected in that world. The Vedas makes frequent reference to the "five classes of people," (RV 1.7.9; 1.89.10; 1.100.12; 1.117.3; 1.176.3; 2.2.10; 3.37.9; 3.53.16; 3.59.8; 4.38.10; 5.32.11; 5.35.12; 5.86.2; 6.11.8; 6.46.7; 6.51.11; 6.61.12; 7.15.2; 7.49.2; 7.72.5; 7.73.5; 7.75.4; 7.79.1; 8.9.2; 8.32.22; 8.52.7; 9.52.7; 9.65.23; 9.66.20; 9.92.3; 9.101.9) which is interpreted as the social division of classes in society. The five classes of people are ruled by members of the Adityas (Astrological Houses):

- The Principle of Change (Agni). (RV 6.11.4; 7.15.2; 9.66.20; 10.45.6.)
- Indra. (RV 1.7.9; 3.7.9; 5.32.11; 5.35.2; 6.41.7; 8.32.22.)
- Indragni. (RV 5.87.2.)
- The Principle of Duality (Asvins). (RV 1.117..3; 7.69.2, 5; 7.73.5; 8.9.2.)
- Mitra. (RV 3.59.8.)
- Aditi. (RV 1.89.10.)
- Spiritual and Mental Wakening. (Usas)(RV 7.75.4; 7.79.1.)
- The Divine Ecstacy of Eternal Union (Soma). (RV 1.176.3; 9.86.29; 9.92.3; 9.101.9.)

The cardinal number five appears in other contexts:

- The five stages of creation. (JB 1.45, 46.)
- The five seasons. (RV 1.164.13; SPB 1.3.5.10, 11; 1.3.2.16; 2.1.1.12; 2.2.3.15; 2.4.4.25; 3.4.1.14; 3.6.4.18; 3.9.4.11; 4.1.1.16; 4.5.5.12; 5.1.2.9; 6.1.2.18; 6.2.2.38; 6.3.1.25; 6.5.1.12; 6.8.1.15, 18; 7.1.1.32, 34; 7.2.3.4; 8.4.1.11, 12; 8.6.3.12; 8.7.4.9; 9.1.1.26; 9.2.2.6; 9.2.3.41; 9.4.2.24; 9.4.4.14; 11.1.6.5; 11.2.6.11; 11.7.4.4; 12.2.2.6, 19; 12.3.2.11; 13.1.7.3; 13.4.4.11.)

- The five regions of the earth wherein the dynamic cosmic law (*rta*) rules. (RV 9.86.29.)
- The five Bulls in heaven, most likely the constellation Taurus. (RV 1.105.10.)

The cardinal number five figures prominently in the eternal law of Sacrifice:

- The Sacrifice is described as "five-fold." (SPB 1.1.2.16; 1.5.2.16; 1 1.5.2.16; 1.5.3.1; 1.7.2.8; 2.1.1.12; 3.1.3.17; 3.1.4.20; 3.2.3.13.)
- The animal sacrifice is called "five-fold." (SPB 1.2.3.7; 1.2.3.8.)
- The five different body parts in the victim at animal sacrifices. (SPB 1.5.2.16; 1.7.2.8; 1.8.1.12; AB 2.14; 3.23.)
- The victim is cut into five pieces. (SPB 1.7.2.8; 1.8.1.12.)
- The five kinds of victims: man, horse, bullock, ram, and he-goat. (AV 11.2.9; SPB 1.2.3.6; 1.7.2.8; 2.1.1.12; 3.1.4.20; 2.3.6.7; 6.2.1.6.18; 7.5.2; TS. 4.2.10.)
- The sacrifice is officiated by five priests, terrestrial and otherwise. (RV 2.34.14; 3.7.7; 5.42.1.)

Five is the cardinal number of the sacrifice and five animals are used as victims because there are five seasons. (SPB 1.5.2.16; 1.7.2.8; 2.2.12; 3.1.4.20; 3.6.4.8; 11.7.4.4; 14.1.2.14.) This is the Vedic version of "Five Easy Pieces," if you will.

Seriously, though, the number Five resonates in many areas, and this resonance is reflected in the Vedic dharma. You may wonder as to the references of five regions. The scriptures make clear that in addition to the four customary regions, there is a fifth region above the bottom four. (SPB 3.2.3.14; 5.4.4.6; 6.1.2.19.) The Five-Dimensional Universe is thus an important layer of the cosmic order. The Five-Dimensional Universe is the gateway to the transcendent Seven-Dimensional Universe. This is most clearly demonstrated in the Yoga Sutras. For example, there are five Yamas, specific mental attitudes to train the mind in the worshiper's dealings with the world: Ahimsa, non-violence or non-harming others or oneself. (YS, 2.35.)

- Satya, truthfulness or honesty to others and oneself. (YS, 2.36.)
- Asteya, non-stealing. (TS, 2.37.)
- Brahmacharya, living oneself life bathed in the awareness of God and the divine. (YS, 2.38.)
- Aparigraha, non-attachment. (YS, 2.39.)

There are also five niyamas, specific inner practices train the mind:

- Shaucha, inner purity of mind and body. (YS, 2.40, 2.41.)
- Santosha, inner contentment. (YS, 2.42.)
- Tapas, the inner austerities, intense meditation. (YS, 2.43.)
- Svadhyaya, study and reflection of the scriptures. (YS, 2.44.)
- Isvarah pranidhana, surrender to God. (YS, 2.45.)

These inner and outer practices condition the five types of mental processes (YS, 1.6):

- Pramana, valid cognition.
- Viparayayah, invalid cognition.
- Vikalpa, imagination.
- Nidra, deep sleep.
- Smirtayah, memory, the act of remembering.

These practices elevate five types of kleshas, thoughts which muddy our thoughts (YS, 2.3):

- Forgetting, ignorance about the nature of things. (YS, 2.5.)
- The sense of I-ness, individuality, ego-ness, Ego. (YS, 2.6.)
- Attachments to mental impressions (samskaras). (YS, 2.7.)
- The aversion to thought patterns or objects. (YS, 2.8.)
- Attachment to thought patterns or material objects as being life itself. (YS, 2.9.)

The material body of the Vedic microcosm, the worshiper, is powered by pranayama, the Vital Air or Life Force. Consistent with this aspect of existence, there are five principal components to the microcosm — prana, apana, vyana, udana, and samana (Vas. S., 2.42 – 45) — the same principal components to pranayama. The practice of pranayama is one of five specific practices to train and focus the mind's attention (YS, 1.34 – 38):

- Focus on breathing awareness.
- Focus on sensation.
- Focus on inner illumination.
- Concentration on a stable mind.
- Focus on the streaming of thoughts of the mind.

The Five-Dimensional Universe has a similar significance to Alchemical Ayurveda. Ayurvedic texts frequently refer to the "killing" of a substance such as gold or mercury. (R., 2.216.) The Vedas and Brahmans also speak of the "killing" of Soma. (K.B., 3.32; SPB 3.2.6.6; 3.9.4.3; 3.9.4.8; 3.9.4.23; 4.3.4.1.) The thought that underlies this process is just as a human being once killed cannot be brought back to life, so a metal or substance once "killed" cannot return to its original, previous state.

Similarly, once conditioned by the practices and insights obtained in the Five-Dimensional Universe, the worshiper is ready to enter the luminosity of the Seven-Dimensional Universe. There, the worshiper integrates and incorporates that blissful state present in the divine Vedic dharma (*rta*).

RV 1.164.14:

The wheel rolls on.
The Ten yoke the wheel upwards.

A MODEST INTERPRETATION:

Many possible interpretations of this rc.

Here the wheel is metaphorical for the fluctuations (vrttis) of the mind. Sayana correctly states that the Ten are the ten sense organs. According to the Samkhya philosophy there are ten sense organs, five for the gross (microcosmic) senses and five for the subtle (macrocosmic) senses. They guide the mind through the intake of information. RV 1.164.11 states that the Principle of Change (Agni) informs the worshiper of the higher wisdom contained in the macrocosm. Rishi Dirghatama indicates that these senses thereby guide the mind upwards, towards that higher consciousness, to the spiritual benefit of the worshiper while traveling on the Vedic path to liberation and salvation. In the Vedic year there were ten, sometimes twelve, months. Another possible interpretation is that the "ten" refers to the ten seasons. That the ten yoke the wheel is a metaphorical representation that time, like Ol' Man River, just keeps rolling along.

The importance this rc (mantra) attaches to time is significant, and somewhat unique.

RV 1.164.15

Of the seven, six are twins and the seventh is
born alone and apart from the others.
The six are placed in their proper position and move, changing form.

A MODEST INTERPRETATION:

Sayana interprets the "six" as being the seasons, which in the Vedic world
each have two months. This is an unlikely interpretation because while
the number of months for the seasons have varied in the Vedic world, six
seasons was never indicative of months. This is a Modest Interpretation:
The "six" refers to the asterisms in the zodiac, which are constantly moving.
The fact they are twins refers to the two hemispheres and give greater
support for this interpretation. The One, the seventh, is the dynamic
cosmic order which set this entire process to operate.

RV 1.164.16

Those [asterisms] that have become females, become male.
The ignorant do not understand this, but
those who can see, the learned, do.

The masculine and feminine in Heaven and Earth
Move around between *zi* (Northern Hemisphere) and *wu.* (Southern Hemisphere)
Cantong qi
Pregadio, The Seal of the Unity of Three, 3.77:13, 14.

A MODEST INTERPRETATION:

Some asterisms are comprised in and influence the female principle, the principle of knowledge and creativity, grounded in the left-handed world, ruled by the Moon, and some are comprised in and influence the male principle, the regenerative principle, which is right handed, ruled by the Sun.

According to Vedic astrology, the masculine, feminine, and neuter characteristics of the asterisms are the following (*http://jyotishvidya.com/nakshatras.htm*):

The asterisms with masculine characteristics are:

- Purnarvsu.
- Pushya.
- Hasta.

- Anuradha.
- Shravana.
- P. Bhadra.
- U. Bhadra.
- Asvini.

The asterisms with the feminine characteristics are:

- Kirtiika.
- Rohini.
- Ardra.
- Aslesha.
- Magha.
- P. Phalguni.
- U. Phalguni.
- Chitra.
- Srati.
- Jyeshtha.
- P. Shada (Ashada).
- U. Shada (Ashada).
- Dhanishtha (Shravishtha).
- Revati.
- Bharani.

The neuter asterisms are:

- Mrgishira.
- Moola (Vichrtau).
- Satabisha.

The asterisms revolve around two hemispheres, the Northern and Southern path. When the Moon and the Sun are conjoined in Dhanishtha (Shravishtha), the male and female roles are switched, and the asterisms move across the two hemispheres. (RVJ 7, 8, Mishra.) In this journey, uttarana, the Northern path which begins at the elliptical point of the winter solstice, moves to its terminal at the vernal equinox, in Mrgishira. The Southern path commences from the vernal equinox to the winter solstice.

RV 1.164.17:

The cow stands up carrying its calf.
Where is it going?
It is going to the herd.

A MODEST INTERPRETATION:

The Sukta changes gears again. Just to make matters a little murkier the Rishii introduces two other symbols: The Cow and the Calf.

Sayana interprets this rc (mantra) as representative of the sacrifice, the cow representing the burnt offering and the calf Agni. Sayana also opines that the cow is the solar rays and the calf is the worship. A Modest Interpretation: The cow represents knowledge which raises the consciousness of the worshiper, the calf. This is interpretation is consistent with Sayana's. The acquisition of knowledge, whether it be self-realization or the understanding of how the worshiper fits in the universe, is the primary goal of the sacrificial rite.

The Veda's preoccupation of all things bovine is extensive and complex. Now is not quite the time to discuss this very important facet of the Asyavamasya Sukta. That discussion is found in RV 1.164.26.

RV 1.164.18:

There are twelve fellies and a single wheel, and there are three naves.
Who can understand this?
Therein are three hundred and sixty spokes which cannot be loosened.

Thirty spokes join one wheel.

Tao Te Ching, 11.

A MODEST INTERPRETATION:

This rc (mantra) continues from the previous. As this passage demonstrates, the preoccupation with Vedic dharma, the Natural Order (*rta*) and the Asyavamasya Sukta was the same: To explain in broad brushes the inner workings of the cosmic order. But whereas Vedic dharma, the Natural Order (*rta*), explains that the thirty spokes, the days consisting in one month, originated from emptiness, the Vedic world is based on an abundant plenum which brings a world full of being and life.

"There are Twelve Fellies"

The Sukta again interprets the number twelve, plus other numbers. They each have their own meaning.

The dynamic cosmic law (*rta*) creates and establishes the months and days of the year. The dynamic divine cosmic order (*rta*) provided for a twelve-month as well as a ten-month year. Twelve also refers to the zodiacal houses and the twelve incarnations of divine union and ecstasy.

"Three Naves"

The "Three Naves" refer to the Three-Dimensional, material, Universe, within which the zodiacal houses and months reside. A little later, in RV 1.164.20, the Asyavamasya Sukta speaks about the Two-Dimensional Universe. The Three-Dimensional Universe in general and the three naves is that space where the polar oppositions of the Two-Dimensional Universe are conjoined, merged, and reconciled. Exactly how are these opposites united?

Agni, in his manifestation as the Principle of Change, reconciles the opposing powers of the Heaven and the Earth. (RV 1.69.1-2; 1.70.1-2; 1.96.2; 1.98.2; 1.143.3; 1.146.2; 1.173.3; 2.2.3, 4;3.3.4, 5; 3.7.1; 3.18.2; 3.55.10; 5.4.1; 5.8.2; 6.7.1;6.9.4; 6.15.14.) This expression is coded language to say that the light of the force of consciousness pervades everything. The force of the light of consciousness is the one factor that pervades the cosmos and everything in the universe. As we learned earlier, the Principle of Change and Transformation (Agni) reconciles the opposing powers of the Sun and the Moon:

- Agni, in his manifestation as the Principle of Change, is identified with the Sun, Surgher, Savitr. (RV 1.57.1; 4.11.1; 3.11.1; 4.13.1.)
- On an astronomical level, Agni, in his manifestation as the Principle of Change, moves the celestial sphere where the sky is fixed, and with the help of the Rishis (stars) leads this sphere like a horse. (RV 3.2.7.)
- In addition, Agni, in his manifestation as the Principle of Change, holds the rim of the celestial sphere that holds the sun. (RV 2.5.1.)
- At the same time, Agni is identified with the moon. (RV 1.24.10; 1.27.6, 11, 12; 1.74.6; 5.101.4; 4.2.12; 4.16.19; 5.6.5; 3.25.3; 5.8.1; 1.6.5, 6; 5.10.4; 5.11.1; 5.61.16.)

In the same way, the Vedic force of Indra, in his manifestation as Force (Bala), possesses these same powers:

- On the one hand, Indra represents the Sun. (RV 4.31.5 - 6, 15.)
- On the other hand, Indra represents the many faces of the Moon, either as the Bright Moon (RV 1.52.9), the Full Moon (RV 1.53.2), the Waning Moon (RV 8.96.1, 4), or the Moon proper. (RV 8.81.9; 9.93.5; 10.134.3.)

By conquering Vrtra Indra melds two of the most visceral, diametrically opposed physical forces, Asat — the indiscriminate mass of non-being, non-existence, anti-matter which pervaded before the appearance of form and shape — and sat, or that being, existence, matter (RV 6.24.5), into living breathing, primordial material, Prakrti. Indra can thus be considered the force of fusion which consists of the almost unlimited power to create energy, fully justifying his epithet as Bala, "Strength." (RV 1.80.8; 3.53.18; 6.47.30; 7.82.2; 9.113.1; 10.54.2; 10.87.25; 10.133.5.)

"Three Hundred and Sixty Spokes"

The "three hundred and sixty spokes" refer to the number of days in a year.

The import of this rc (mantra) is the year as influenced by the asterisms in the zodiac. How did the Rishii arrive at this number? It would be too easy to say that the answer is provided in the next rc. It is not. Look to RV 1.168.42. In the meantime, ….

RV 1.164.19:

That which descends will ascend, and that which ascends will descend.
Conjunction and unity (Indra) in conjunction with
Divine Ecstacy (Soma) create the regions.
They carry the rays of light to travel in the far
reaches of the space like yoked horses.

The crippled becomes whole
The crippled becomes straight
Hollow becomes full
Worn becomes new
Little becomes more
Much becomes delusion
Therefore, Sages cling to the One
And take care of this world.

Tao Te Ching, 22.

One aspect of the Vedic dharma (*rta*) focuses on Opposition, and the conjoining of opposites, and emphasizes the ultimate unity of the world despite these opposites. This is the subject of this rc (mantra).

A MODEST INTERPRETATION:

"That which descends will ascend, and that which ascends will descend."

This rc (mantra) reiterates (begins?) the First Law of occult philosophy, articulated so eloquently in the Emerald Tablet: "As above, so below." "That which" is not identified, but there is no lack of interpretation. According to Sayana this discusses the relative movements of the planets, asterisms, and of the houses of the zodiac. Sayana posits that Conjunction and Unity (Indra) creates the regions through which "that which" travel. Other interpretations identify the "that which" as rays of light. It is for the reader to decide. For the purposes of the Vedic dharma, the undulating ascending and descending movements are the upward and downward movements of the Saman chant discussed in the Chandogya Upanishad as discussed.

"Conjunction And Unity (Indra) In Conjunction With Divine Ecstacy (Soma) Create The Regions."

The rc (mantra) says that Indra and Soma create the "regions" (read: the cosmos) but does not say how. It is through the Articulation of Mind and Matter.

Without Speech no form could exist. (SB, 2.5.) Without speech, any form could not be known, and the worshiper would be bereft of intelligence. Having obtained information from the sensory organs, the worshiper obtains (SA, 5.7):

- all names, through smell all odors through speech with intelligence,
- all sounds, through the tongue with intelligence all taste through sight with intelligence all forms, through hearing with intelligence,
- all feeling, through the body with intelligence all pleasure and pain through the hands with intelligence,
- all "dalliance" and joy through the generative organ with intelligence,

- all motion through the feet with intelligence, and
- all thoughts through the mind with intelligence.

Without speech, the worshiper would not know these odors, sounds, tastes, pleasure or pain, joy, motion or thoughts. (SA, 5.3; 5.6.) Much like the Tommy character in the Who's rock opera, the worshiper is "deaf, dumb, and blind."

Indra represents the Strength of Intelligence and is made sensible in the Articulation of Mind and Matter. What is the basis for this intelligence? Indra is breath, and when the nose smell, hands feel, eyes see, or mind thinks, breath follows closely thereto. (SA, 5.8.) For this reason, Breath alone is intelligence (SA, 5.2), and Indra is that intelligence, reflected as Truth. (SA, 5.3.) In this manifestation Indra (SA, 5.1):

- Articulates all names.
- Establishes all smells and odors.
- Molds all forms.
- Carries all sounds.
- Installs in the mind all thoughts.

In his manifestation of Articulation and Breath Indra performs these five functions. Not to get too wrapped up in Numerology, but the fact that this manifestation has five functions is significant. In this manifestation of Articulation and Breath, Indra performs these powers within the auspices of the Five-Dimensional Universe.

Yet, Indra has an on-going struggle with Vrtra. There is no image in all Vedic literature more enduring that the serpent Vrtra slain by Indra after consuming Soma.

We were introduced to Vrtra earlier. Vrtra is representative of ignorance, avidya. Vrtra's name is indeed derived from the combination of the Sanskrit root of "to cover or obscure" and *rta*, the Natural Order (i.e., v + Rta = vrtra). Ignorance, through the agency of Vrtra, covers the truth. More importantly, Vrtra covers the mystic significance of the natural law (*rta*), the cosmic laws of the universe and obscures that meaning to the Worshiper. Thus, Vrtra's function is to cover, obscure, hide and conceal the information by which the worshiper can make intelligible the universe or the cosmic laws from which the universe operates. Vrtra and all it represents is a barrier to liberation.

Just as enduring is the image of the results of Vrtra's death. Vrtra obstructs and conceals the waters. (RV 2.54.10; 1.57.4; 1.62.11 (Vala); 1.61.10; 1.80.10; 2.14.2; 2.30.2; 3.33.6; 4.16.7; 5.20.2; 8.12.26; 9.61.22; 10.113.6.) The waters, as we saw in earlier chapters, has many metaphorical, esoteric meanings. In this context, the occult meanings of waters are:

- They are metaphorical for purification.
- They are reflective of the process of evolution and dissolution, that process which accounts for the cycle of the process of creation, its eventual dissolution, and its subsequent evolution.
- They represent the Vedic dharma taken as a whole.
- They are also symbolic of the spiritual, mental, and psychological rewards brought by Indra, obtained as the result of the victory over Vrtra.

When Indra, as the Articulation of Mind and Matter, slays Vrtra after drinking Soma, he uncovers the full import of the seven Eternal Laws, fosters the purification of the soul, and brings the spiritual, mental, and psychological benefits of the worshiper's mind and soul. Indra is the Articulation of Mind and Matter, uncovering this sensory data by the slaying of Vrtra. This is displayed by the very language of the Veda.

- RV 2.11.2; 2.22.4, Indra releasing the waters.
- RV 4.17.1, Indra feed the waters arrested by Vala.
- RV 6.17.12, Indra freed the rivers and the waters.
- RV 1.56.6, under the influence of Soma, Indra released the waters after killing Vrtra with a rock.
- RV 1.61.1, Indra releases the nourishing waters.
- RV 1.80.5, Indra smote Vrtra impelling the waters to flow.
- RV 1.54.10, Indra slew Vrtra and released the waters.
- RV 1.80.4, Indra released waters concealed by Vrtra.
- RV 1.32.10, 11, Indra released the waters concealed in darkness.
- RV 3.33.7, Indra tore Ahi asunder releasing the waters.

- RV 4.17.3, Indra shattered the mountain of Vrtra with Vrtra releasing the waters.
- RV 6.17.12, Indra released the waters into the ocean.
- RV 4.19.6, Indra gave birth to the universal streams and allowed the waters to flow.

The Waters relate to the essence of the Vedic dharma; that essence informs the consciousness which pervades in the dharma; that consciousness informs the Knowledge the worshiper seeks to gain to vanquish ignorance. In conquering ignorance, Vrtra, Indra creates a higher level of Consciousness. When Vrtra is slain, Indra, in his manifestations of Articulation, Breath, and Matter, releases these spiritual tools that are used by the worshiper in the path towards liberation and salvation:

- In his manifestations of Articulation, Breath, and Matter, Indra releases or is the giver of the waters (spiritual purity). (RV 1.32.1, 2; 1.33.11, 12; 1.51.11; 1.52.2, 6, 8, 10, 14; 1.54.4; 1.57.2, 6; 1.59.6; 1.61.10, 12; 1.80.2, 5, 10; 1.125.5; 1.130.3; 1.131.4; 1.169.8; 1.174.2, 4; 2.11.5; 2.20.7; 2.30.1; 3.30.9, 10; 3.31.20; 3.32.5, 6, 11; 3.33.6; 3.38.5; 3.45.2; 3.51.9; 5.30.5; 5.31.6; 5.33.6.)
- In his manifestations of Articulation, Breath, and Matter, Indra releases or is the giver of the seven rivers (Seven eternal laws). (See RV 1.32.6; 2.12.3; 4.8.7 (Indra releases the rivers); 6.17.12 (releases the rivers and the waters); 1.32.1 1 - 15; 2.13.5; 4.19.5, 8; 4.28.1 (seven rivers feed with Soma's friendship); 3.33.6; 6.18.24 (released after slaying Vudhyamadhi). See also, 4.19.2 - 5 (Vrtra besieged the waters and stretched against the seven rivers).)
- In his manifestations of Articulation, Breath, and Matter, Indra releases or is the giver of the ordinary rivers, symbolic for the stream of mental consciousness present in perceptive awareness. (RV 2.12.3; 1.33.11; 1.62.6; 1.83.1; 1.102.2; 1.174.9; 1.181.6; 4.17.1; 4.19.2, 6, 7, 8; 4.22.6.)
- Indra, in his manifestations of Articulation, Breath, and Matter, releases or is the giver of the cows (knowledge). (RV 2.12.3; 2.14.3; 2.19.3; 2.20.5; 2.24.3, 6; 2.30.7; 3.30.14, 20, 21; 3.31.8; 3.44.5; 3..47.4; 3.38.7; 3.39.6; 3.50.3; 4.9.7;4.17.10, 11; 4.20.8; 4.22.5;

4.24.1; 5.45.1; 5.86.4; 6.17.3; 1.32.1 - 15 (released the ray-cows and waters).)

- Indra, in his manifestations of Articulation, Breath, and Matter, releases or is the giver of the dawn (mental understanding and awareness) and the rivers. (RV 4.19.8; 7.21.3.)
- In his manifestations of Articulation, Breath, and Matter, Indra) releases or removes the clouds (mental doubt or anguish). (RV 1.7.6; 2.17.1; 8.7.23 (releases the "mountain mists.").) According to the Vedic scholar R.L. Kashyap, the esoteric meaning of "clouds" is the active movements of the mind which cover the inner light, analogous to the vritti.
- In his manifestations of Articulation, Breath, and Matter, Indra releases or is the giver of light (Truth). (RV 1.42.2; 1.100.8; 2.12.3; 2.11.18; 2.14.3; 2.21.4; 2.24.3, 6; 3.30.14, 20, 21; 3.34.4.; 3.38.7; 3.39.7; 4.19.7; 4.22.5, 10; 5.42.18; 8.45.19.)
- In his manifestations of Articulation, Breath, and Matter, Indra is the Lord of the Cattle, metaphoric language for Knowledge or the Mind. (RV 1.101.4; 3.21.4; 4.24.1; 7.86.6; 10.108.3.)

These waters are released when they flow to the ocean, their place of origin. (RV 6.17.12.) In the stylized, coded, language of the Rg Veda, this simile of the Ocean states the bedrock of Vedanta philosophy that when the veil of ignorance is lifted, the individual I-Consciousness begins to be absorbed into the Universal Self, the paratman. It is a symbol and meaning repeated in many ways throughout the Vedas.

This portion of the rc, then, addresses the events before and after the worlds are created, or more precisely, when the intelligent mind, through the agency of Indra and Soma, finds the words needed to perceive and articulate that world.

RV 1.164.20:

There are two birds sitting on a tree.
One is eating, and the other one is not eating but merely looks around.

A MODEST INTERPRETATION:

Sayana interprets the two birds in this rc (mantra) as the individual soul, the jiva (the bird eating) and the other bird sitting and looking as the Supreme Spirit, the Atman. This is a common, accepted interpretation.

This rc (mantra) however must be read with reference to the preceding rcs. When this is done the two birds may be interpreted as the upward and downward movements of the Saman chant, or any other characteristic found in the Two-Dimensional Universe.

The number two is a cardinal number in the Vedic dharma. When the One created the multiplicity of forms, it created the Two-Dimensional Universe. The Two-Dimensional Universe is the material world itself. This universe is premised on opposites. As soon as the One is established, its opposite appears. (Richard Wilhelm, *Understanding the I Ching*, p. 157.) Once it arrives, the opposite moves to return to its counterpart. It is a process that does not have a beginning and goes on forever. This is the Two-Dimensional Universe.

The microcosm is interpreted as a binary, Two-Dimensional Universe. The Two-Dimensional Universe is the gateway to the material universe. What is seen, heard, felt and experienced is done so through the prism of the Two-Dimensional Universe. It is the substrate of the sensible world as experienced by the worshiper/subject.

There is a deeper aspect to duality. According to the Pythagoreans, the binary numbers, one and two, represent the subtle essence of the world. The Monad, the unitary Ekam, and Duad, the Two-Dimensional Universe, was the essence of Plato's Unwritten Doctrine. This Unwritten Doctrine was not unknown to the Rishiis of the Vedas or other ancient knowledge. The two binary numbers, one and two and their combinations, is the foundation of the mathematical laws that inhabit a priori existence. These binary numbers and their combinations represent the unassailable spiritual order that is "completely self-contained and leaves no room for anything equivocal or half-way in between." (Richard Wilhelm, *Understanding the I Ching*, p. 101.)

The Vedic forces ruling over the Two-Dimensional Universe are the two Asvins, NaSatya and Dasra. The Asvins are the Vedic forces closely associated with Indra in his manifestations of the Power of Conjunction, Unity and Knowledge. The Asvins represent divine duality, the subtle basis for all forms of duality. While the philosophical undercurrent of the Vedas is nondual, the divine duality of the Asvins is a synergistic whole constantly interacting between themselves, much as the alternating current of electricity. "Nasatya" means "rapid movement" (Kashyap, Commentary, RV 1.3.3) and "Dasra" means "enlightened giving." These attributes are communicated to Indra, in his manifestations of the Power of Conjunction and Unity. Indra is energized thereby to create the multiplicity of forms in the world. (RV 3.53.8; 6.47.18.) The sensible universe is made manifest in this manner, the Asvins giving rise to the duality present in the sensible world.

For the Vedas, the binary nature of the Two-Dimensional Universe reflects the primordial opposing forces operating in the Vedic material world. These opposing Vedic forces include:

- The Southern and Northern paths upon which the worshiper's soul travels after death.
- The contracting, uniting and conjoining powers of Indra protecting all sentient beings from the perils of evil (RV 8.24.6), and the left-handed powers of Conjunction and Unity (Indra) bringing spiritual blessings. (RV 8.81.6.)

- Light and Dark. Light, representing self-realizing knowledge and divinity, the Samkhya formulation of Sattva, and Darkness, representing ignorance, matter and materiality, the Samkhya formulation of tamas.
- Heaven and Earth.
- The Sun and the Moon.
- Day and Night.
- Sat (RV 1.23.15; 1.164.46; 2.41.10; 3.56.2; 4.5.10; 6.18.4; 6.27.2; 7.18.4; 8.68.14; 8.73; 9.61.10; 10.72.2; 10.129.1) and asat. (RV 1.9.5; 1.89.5; 1.114.1; 1.143.6; 1.173.9; 1.186.3; 1.186.3; 3.23.3; 6.23.10; 6.34.5; 7.53.3; 7.85.4; 8.31.18; 10.129.1; 10.137.10; 10.189.1.)

The Two-Dimensional Universe is limited and limiting. There is no physical, mental or spiritual progression in a Two-Dimensional Universe. Like a debate between two speakers, one advocates one position while the other advocates its counter-position. There is no resolution, and the elements are mired in constant conflict, endless discussion. The Two-Dimensional Universe is Maya in action. Stuck between these opposing forces, the worshiper is found truly "between the devil and the deep blue sea." The spiritual progress is minimal or nonexistent. The Two-Dimensional Universe operates back and forth, back and forth. In terms of the worshiper's spiritual increase it is an endless cycle of transmigration where the soul is stuck forever being reborn, never achieving liberation.

In the Vedic path to liberation and salvation, spiritual development is achieved in three ways.

- One, these opposing forces are united, which is discussed further in a later chapter.
- Two, the perpetual conflict is resolved in the give-and-take of the sacrifice.
- Three, any resolution, and consequent mental and spiritual progress, is achieved in the conjoining of opposites in the Three-Dimensional Universe.

The Two-Dimensional Universe is premised on the Left and Right Movements of vibration. The left is the blessed side, consecrated by Indra's manifestation as Divine Grace; the right side is the movement of discernment. That which eats the fruit of the tree is blessed; the other bird sits in discernment. The dichotomous dual movements are a fitting reflection of the material world, but only one part of the Vedic dharma (*rta*).

RV 1.164.21:

There where the birds sing the Lord Protector of all enters me,
ignorant though I am, and I attain wisdom.

A MODEST INTERPRETATION:

This is the point where the worshiper achieves liberation and salvation.
This is the attainment of discrimination where the worshiper realizes that
he is the Atman (the eating bird) while at the same time a sitting bird (the
universal Atman).

RV 1.164.22:

On that tree the birds rest, inspiring each other.
On the top of the tree are berries.
If one does not reach the top of the tree,
one does not reach the Father.

A MODEST INTERPRETATION:

Sayana's interpretation of the two birds is inconsistent when read with this rc. Another meaning must be found.

Consider: The "Father" here is Pitr, more accurately translated as "decedent" or "forefather." The Land of the Forefathers is contrasted with the Land of the Gods, devayana, the Land of the Gods, which is the spiritual goal of the worshiper. It is there, Land of the Gods, that the worshiper achieves liberation and is saved, and is blessed not to transmigrate to this sensible world, the Land of the Forefathers, again. That the father, then, is here represented as being located at the top of the tree is, to say the least, counterintuitive. Then a meaning must be found for the word "tree" as used in this rc. The Katha Upanishad speaks of the world as being a tree. (K. Up. 3.1.)

In Orion or the Antiquity of the Vedas, Gangabhar Tilak states that in the early Vedic days the year — and the dates scheduled for the yearly sacrifices — commenced when the Sun was located at the Vernal Equinox as the Sun progressed northward from the southern hemisphere. (Tilak, pp. 24 - 26.) This was associated with the devayana, the realm of the Gods.

When the Sun travels north it is among the Gods, says the Satapatha Brahmana. (SPB, 2.1.2.1 - 3.)

And yet there was a lack of agreement as to what constituted "North." The Vedanga Jyotisha notes that the year commenced at the winter solstice (RVJ, 5) and the beginning of the year and the sacrificial rites began at that time. Tilak concluded that at some point in time this orientation changed. It is very possible that RV 1.164.22 refers to that tradition following the Vedanga Jyotisha. It is possible that RV 1.164.22 refers to a tradition that is much older than either the Vedanga Jyotisha or the Satapatha Brahmana. It is also possible that consistent with this interpretation, the two birds represent the two hemispheres of the asterisms.

Other interpretations abound, of course. Geldner, a 19th Century Vedic scholar, interprets this rc (mantra) as symbolizing the attainment of knowledge. As the Asyavamasya Sukta implies, Who really knows?

RV 1.164.23:

Those who understand that how Gayatri, Tristup
or Jagati are based attain immortal life.

A MODEST INTERPRETATION:

Another overarching principle in the Natural Order, *rta*, is Breath,
otherwise known as prana, or wind. This rc (mantra) deals with the Vedic
translation of prana as Saman.

The next three rcs deal with the rhythms and metres with which the
hymns and chants at the sacrifice are recited. The import of this rc (mantra)
is that the secret of immortality is contained deep in the sacrificial chant,
and once the full appreciation of the progression of the rhythms and meters
of the sacrificial chant are uncovered, immortality is the result.

We should step back for a moment to examine exactly what this
rc (mantra) promises. Vedic and Hindu literature are framed in coded
language, and so is the language here. "Immortality" in RV 1.164.23,
indeed, "immortality," whenever that word occurs in the Vedas,
Upanishads, or yogic texts, no more means that the worshiper will live
forever as are the numerous references in Hatha yoga scriptures that the
asanas will "cheat death." "Immortality" and "cheating death" are coded
words meaning that the worshiper will achieve some measure of salvation
and/or liberation. This rc (mantra) indicates, therefore, that somehow as
a result of understanding how the rhythms and meters of the sacrificial
chant progress, that understanding will assist the worshiper in the Vedic
journey to liberation and salvation.

Passages from the Satapatha Brahmana (SPB 9.1.2.32 – 35) provides a clue to the meaning of this rc (mantra):

31. With seven (formulas) he draws them across, – the altar consists of seven layers, and seven seasons are a year, and Agni is the year: as great as Agni is, as great as is his measure, with so much he thus crosses him. Having thrown the cane on the heap of rubbish; –

32. [The Adhvaryu] then sings hymns round it (the altar); – for therein that whole Agni is completed; and the gods laid into him that highest form, immortality; and in like manner does this (Sacrificer) thereby lay into him that highest form, immortality. Saman-hymns are (used), for samans are vital airs, and the vital airs are immortality: immortality, that highest form, he thus lays into him. On every side he sings around it: everywhere he thus lays immortality, that highest form, into him.

33. And, again, as to why he sings Saman-hymns round about it;–the gods then desired, 'Let us make this body of ours boneless and immortal.' They spake, 'Think ye upon this, how we may make this body of ours boneless and immortal!' They spake, 'Meditate (kit) ye!' whereby indeed they meant to say, 'Seek ye a layer (kriti)! seek ye how we may make this body of ours boneless and immortal!

34. Whilst meditating, they saw those Saman-hymns, and sang them round about it, and by means of them they made that body of theirs boneless and immortal; and in like manner does the Sacrificer, when he sings the Saman-hymns round about it, make that body of his boneless and immortal. On every side he sings: everywhere he thus makes that body of his boneless and immortal. Standing he sings, for these worlds stand, as it were; and whilst standing one doubtless is stronger. He sings, after uttering (the syllable) 'him,' for therein the Saman-hymn becomes whole and complete.

35. He first sings the Gayatra hymn for the Gayatri metre is Agni: he thus makes Agni his head, and that head of his (or of him, Agni) he thus makes boneless and immortal.

These passages demonstrate important aspects of Vedic sacrifice and begin to explain the meaning of this rc. It demonstrates the give-and-take of the Vedic sacrifice. Notice, the gods wanted to be immortal, so who do they ask? The Adhvaryu, the Vedic priest. The Adhvaryu commences to meditate, chants, becomes immortal and confers that immortality to the gods. Note, that immortality was achieved through chanting. There must be something then inherent in the act of chanting which creates a state of mind where the seeds of salvation may grow.

Still, these foregoing passages still do not fully explain the import of this rc, nor does it fully explain the process by which the understanding of the meter progression leads to liberation and salvation. In addition, it does not address the principal focus of the Asyavamasya Sukta: the explanation of the dynamic cosmic order and how the worshiper fits in this order.

On a deep, esoteric level *rta*, the sacrifice, is the representation of the universe, with its own movement and sequence of events. *Rta*, the dynamic energy of cosmic order, is sacrifice. *Rta* is also the saman, the hymns and chanting recited during the sacrifice. (RV 1.147.1.) There is a reflexive equivalence between *rta*, which is in the nature of sacrifice, yagna, and saman. (RV 8.25.4.)

Vibration is both the subtle aspect of energy which permeates everything in the world and its physical manifestation. On a sub-atomic level it is reflected in the movement of atoms, and is present in the saman, chanting, in the sacrifice. The aspect of Divine Duality (the Asvins) assists the power and energy of Divine grace and Knowledge (Indra) which gives rise to the Right and Left-Handed movements of the universe, and sama is the sacrificial representation of this movement (vibration). Sama is responsible for making all objects in the universe visible. (TB, 2.2.8.7.) The movements of sama undulate with the outward and inward breathes of prana while the hymns are chanted or otherwise; sama also travels inward and outward, rhythmically, as the chanter performs the sama song or mantra. The physical manifestations of these expansion and contraction movements are profound and are reflected in a variety of ways:

- As sound vibrations of musical notes traveling through the air.
- Affect the vibration of the air around and about the chanter.

- Affect the upward and downward aspirations affected both the inner prana of the chanter and the air around him as the chant is recited.
- On a subtle level the vibration affects the psychological demeanor of the chanter and those around the chanter. The vibrations of the uttered chants literally regulate the neurons and psychological and mental states of the chanter and the worshipers.

Thus, the Sama chant creates the environment for both the microcosm, represented by the Saman Chanter, and the macrocosm, the air around him and beyond.

The discussion thereby goes full circle. The Vedic dharma (*rta*) operates by pure vibration at every level. This vibration of Vedic dharma (*rta*) is aptly represented in the Sama chant. From the Vedic dharma, to the metres, to the worshiper, the sacrificial chant pervades all and regulates all creation. These vibrations are represented in the sacrifice by the sama chant. When hearing these chants, the worshiper should allow the chanting to similarly permeate every cell of the mind, body and soul, thereby channeling into the energy of the Vedic dharma (*rta*). A true understanding and implementation of this process will result in the liberation and salvation of the worshiper, or, in the words of this rc, immortality.

RV 1.164.24:

At the sacrifice the prayers are constructed in a Gayatri metre.
The saman chant is constructed in the Tristup metre.
The verses are in Anubaak metre.
One syllable consists of seven metres.

A MODEST INTERPRETATION:

This rc (mantra) continues the discussion of the sacrificial chant and its application to the Vedic dharma.

On one level this rc (mantra) is a short primer on the role of metre at the sacrifice (yajna). Life is sacrifice, and the sacrificial rite is emblematic of the rhythms which permeate every space of the universe. On a deeper level, the saman chants are amplified and incorporated in the physical vibration present in the universe, which reflects the cosmic order (*rta*). The cosmic order is described as the one syllable which is fueled by the seven metres of the saman chant. The seven metres represent the seven levels of the universe.

The Udgitr is the chanter who sings the samans of the SamaVeda. Samana is the portion of prana which balances the prana with the apana. The samans themselves are sung in different meters. There are four principle meters:

- Gayatri, containing three padas and eight syllables;
- Tristubh, containing four padas, and eleven syllables;

- Jagati, containing four 4 padas, and twelve syllables; and
- Anustabh, containing four padas, and eight syllables.

The significance in this correspondence is that samana serves a regulatory and governing function of prana, and thus occupies a higher position, just as the SamaVeda occupies a higher position among the Vedas in containing the distillation of the Rg Veda's slotras. The correspondences between these meters of saman, a person and the senses used to perceive the sensible world are the following (SB, 2.3.7)

Head	Smell	Gayatri
Chest	Sight	Tristubh
Waist	Hearing	Jagati
Feet	Voice	Anustabh

The third column refers to the different meters in which the Rg Vedic hymns. The anthropomorphic correspondence in this chart refer first to the outer surface and then to the sense organs of the microcosmic Purusa, a fancy term for individual person. Esoterically, these correspondences provide the explanation of how the sensible universe originated. Prana may be considered the life energy of all subtle and gross objects. The third column referring to the Vedic meters demonstrate the interplay between Saman and prana, materially appearing as chanting and breathing. It is through the interplay of prana and sama that objects become sensible in the world. (TB, 2.2.8.7.) Sama emits prana at the yajna. (SB, 1.3.21.) Sama so emits prana from the upward and downward movements of the Sama chant. At the yajna, the Udgitr "connects the eye" to the outer world by making two syllables brilliant and connecting them with prana. (SB, 2.1.45.) Whoever meditates on the Udgitha (Om) becomes the possessor of food and the enjoyer of food. This is coded language meaning that the meditator becomes both the Subject and the Object. Through Sama, then, all objects thereby become sensible. In this process and through the meters of saman the subtle world of the Vedic dharma become visible.

RV 1.164.25:

The flowing water is established in heaven by the Jagati metre.
The Sun rests everywhere in Rathantar.
There are three parts to Gayatri.
It is the superior metre.

A MODEST INTERPRETATION:

This rc (mantra) continues the discussion in RV 1.164.24.

"Rathantar" is a type of saman chant. There is a mystical side to the sama chant. A good portion of the Chandogya Upanishad is devoted to the mystical meaning of saman. That meaning is a physical vibration that exists in the universe and it is found in the movements of sound waves. That vibration is represented in the sacrificial context by the sama chant.

The "three parts" of the Gayatri metre is somewhat of a mystery. There are three degrees of vibration in the vibration in the gayatri metre. This rc (mantra) could be a reference to the three constituent elements of the Gayatri metre. The gayatri metre is based on triads. (SPB 1.2.5.6.) Gayatri contains three padas. All of this corresponds to the Three-Dimensional Universe of the material world. The gayatri metre is the superior metre because it is associated with Agni. (SPB 1.3.4.6; 1.3.5.4.) The gayatri metre regulates a specific aspect of the Vedic dharma (*rta*).

The Vedic force of Agni is based on triads. The triple nature of Agni is expressed in other ways, in a simple three-sided geometrical form and triads. In Agni is reposed in the Three Goddesses. (RV 1.13.9; 2.3.8.) The Three Goddesses will appear later as a terrestrial manifestation of Agni.

- Agni as the Sacrificial Fire has three heads and seven rays. (RV 1.146.1.)
- Agni the Sacrificial Fire represents the unifying force of the three existential levels of Heaven, Mid-Earth, and Earth. (RV 10.88.3.)
- In this way, Agni in his aspect as the Fire Altar, with Stamobhaga bricks, twenty-one bricks, is used to symbolize the three worlds and the regions. (SPB 8.5.3.5, 6.)
- These three regions represent the three principal manifestations of the Fire of Change (Agni): Celestial, the "Middle" Agni, and Terrestrial Agni. (BD, 1.91, TB 1.2.1.56, 57.)

As with Agni, the gayatri is also is associated with the earth. (SPB 1.7.2.15.) That principle of flux and change runs through the material world and regulates the passing of the years, thus insuring another year will commence upon the conclusion of the previous and a new morning will be the beginning of a new day after the dawning. The gayatri metre glorifies this perpetuation of the Vedic dharma and everything which is subject to the Vedic dharma or the Natural Oder (*rta*).

According to this rc (mantra) the jagati metre regulates the atmosphere. The jagati metre also establishes water. This is a reference of rain falling from the upper atmosphere. Its association with the metre chanted at the sacrifice is puzzling. Not so puzzling when it is realized that chanting involves the use of the vocal chords and the upward and downward progression of air.

In the Veda, water flows not only downward but also upward. There are plenty of references of water flowing down, as water should. (RV 1.20.2; 1.32.2; 1.52.7; 1.54.7; 1.85.3; 1.174.9; 1.181.3; 2.13.2; 2.25.4; 5.53.2; 5.85.5; 8.32.25.) Amazingly, there are also references of water flowing up. For example,

- The waters flow above to Indra. (RV1.32.8.)
- The mighty power of Bala (Indra) made the stream flow upwards. (RV 2.15.6, 8.)
- A comparison is made between the flow of the river and the ascending powers of Purification and Theosis (Soma). (RV 9.50. 1, 2.)

- References of the uplifted udder of an oblation eating cow. (RV 9.71.4.)
- The splendors of Awareness (Usas) flowing up to heaven. (RV 6.65.2.)

So, while all chanting involves the mechanics of upward and downward progression of air, the Jagati metre, for whatever reason, has been identified as that metre which is associated with this aspect of the generation of water.

RV 1.164.26:

I call the cow that is easily milked, that I may
use one good hand to milk her.
May Savitr produce superior milk for us.

A MODEST INTERPRETATION:

Rishi Dirghatama returns to expand on the nature of and quest for knowledge. While Surya is the source and principle of Energy, this rc (mantra) identifies the nature of Savitr as the source and principle of Knowledge. Savitr is associated with the Sun. As the Sun is a source of all life, Savitr is the source of all knowledge. Cows are said to be symbolic of the primal light (RV 4.36.4), because they produce ghee, or ghrta, the light of consciousness. The cow also produces milk, the milk of knowledge. The worshiper therefore calls on the cow to obtain that knowledge.

The Rg Veda is a book of Knowledge but is more specifically a Book of Symbols. This rc introduces us to an important symbol in the Vedic dharma — the Cow. It is here where the Asyavamasya Sukta delves into what this humble interpreter calls "Bovine Knowledge." The Cow is normally a very placid mammal, interested more in chewing its cud than in anything else. It takes a lot to infuriate a cow, and once riled, quickly calms down. The ancients no doubt superimposed their own aspiration to emulate the cow's demeanor. Its stoic calm indisputably belied a deeper understanding which stood as a stark contrast to the great penchant for mischief in humans.

The cow, however, represents more than an animal. The ancients ascribed a variety of meanings to the general, collective, plural word for "Cows."

• Cows, *gobhir*, signify the winds that blow rain clouds to different areas of the sky. (RV 1.7.3.)

• Cows represent dawn's light which disperse the darkness of light. (RV 1.62.5; 5.74.4; 6.64.3.)

• Cows are invoked to welcome the Asvins, the twin Vedic forces which represent the Divine Duad of the Two-Dimension Universe. (RV 10.61.4.)

• Cows are likened to the rain which replenishes the Earth, symbolizing the spiritual endowment of nourishment. (RV 10.99.4.)

• Cow also symbolize the water used to be mixed with the Soma juice at the Soma Sacrifice, which is later consumed by the worshiper. (RV 9.86.47.)

• Cows are mentioned to represent the heat of the Sun which creates the water vapors which eventually rises up to the clouds. (RV 7.36.1.)

• The Cows represent clarified butter, ghee, or ghrta, which, as we will see, contains a host of its own meanings. (RV 5.3.2.)

• In another sacrificial setting, the Cows represent the milk which is infused with barley flour to prepare mead. (RV 8.2.3.)

The Cows, not surprisingly, represent various items made out of leather. While there is a pedestrian meaning to this aspect of Cows, they all refer to items like the leather straps and joists used in chariots in the chariot simile used in the Katha Upanishad. (RV 6.47.11.) The Cows also refer to the leather used for the leather string for the bow. (RV 8.20.8.) The cow, however, represents more than an animal. The ancients attributed a greater level of knowledge to the cow than meets the eye. The cows represent knowledge, wisdom and illumination, most likely because these qualities are representative of their products: milk, butter and ghee. Because the cows produce several by-products, different cows in the Vedas represent different aspects of knowledge or the mind:

- A barren or immature cow is taken to mean the lack of consciousness, incomplete or faulty knowledge, because of its unripe milk. (RV 3.30.14 (unripe milk); 2.7.5; 1.112.3; 1.116.22; 1.117.20; 1.61.9 (raw cows); 6.72.4; 4.19.7; 7.68.8.)
- The ray-cows represent Aditi, the infinite consciousness. (RV 4.58.4; 4.1.6.)
- The Ray-Cows also represent hidden or occult knowledge. (RV 4.53; 4.58; 4.5.10.)
- A cow's calf represents the Knowledge of the jiva, or the individual soul. (RV 4.33.4; 4.34.5; 1.110.8; 1.111.1; 1.164.5; 1.164.9, 17, 18, 27; 2.7.5; 2.16.8; 2.28.6; 2.24.8; 3.33.3; 3.41.5; 1.55.'4; 6.45.25; 5.30.10; 7.87.5; 8.43.17; 8.59.14, 15; 8.61.5; 9.41.14; 9.86.2; 9.100.1,7; 9.104.2; 9.105.2; 9.111.14; 10.8.2, 9; 10.53.11; 10.119.4; 10.145.6; 10.10.75.4;10.123.1.)

The Cow contains the full panoply of meaning for Knowledge, is far-reaching and extensive. Its meaning implicates not only the Vedic dharma, the Natural Order, but other foundational Vedic concepts.

- Cows represent the inner illumination of the rays of knowledge. (RV 2.24.6.)
- The glory of the cow of light is discovered after meditation of the supreme name of the milch cow. (RV 4.1.16.)
- Cows also represent consciousness as knowledge. (RV 3.30.20; 3.39.6.) Indra finding meath (empirical knowledge) in the cows. (RV 3.31.10; 3.31.11.)
- Cows represent Inspired Knowledge. (RV 10.92.10.)
- According to Sri Aurobindo, cows represent the power of consciousness, discrimination, and discernment. (RV 3.31.11; 10.92.10.) In recognition of this meaning, some English translations render gobhir, as "Ray-Cows," signifying the rays of knowledge. (RV 1.7.3; 1.16.9; 1.23.15; 1.53.4; 1.62.5; 1.95.8; 1.151.8; 2.15.4; 2.30.7, 20; 2.35.8; 3.1.12; 3.50.3; 3.3.3, 4; 8.7; 2.24.6; 2.20.5; 6.19.12; 6.45.20, 24. 6.66.8; 6.64.3 (red rays); 10.92.10; 4.5.5; 4.17.11; 4.23.10; 4.27.5; 4.30.22 (Indra, lord of the ray-cows); 4.31.14; 4.32.6, 7, 18, 22; 4.40.5; 4.42.5; 4.57.1;

5.1.3; 5.2.5;5.3.2; 5.45.8; 5.80.3; 6.44.12; 6.47.27; 6.53.10; 3.55.8; 3.30.10, 21; 2.55.8; 3.35.8; 1.36.8; 9.31.5; 6.1.12 (herds of light); 6.17.2; 6.17.6.; 6.43.3 (ray-cows within the rock); 6.28.1 (ray-cows bringing bliss); 6.28.3; 9.31.5 (ray cows yielding light and the milk of knowledge); 7.18.2; 7.41.3; 7.54.2; 7.90.2; 8.2.6; 8.20.8; 8.24.6; 9.62.12 (Soma pours the ray-cows and life-energies upon us) The "Ray-Cows" of Sri Aurobindo perfectly crystallizes the symbolism and significance of the Cow, a well-known phrase — the Cow represents the *Rays* of Knowledge.

- Gobhir, the ray-cows, figured prominently in the Ninth Mandala, is the presiding divinity of Soma Pavamana. (RV 9.2.4; 9.6.6; 9.8.5; 9.10.3; 9.14.3; 9.32.3; 9.43.1; 9.50.5; 9.61.13; 9.66.13; 9.68.9; 9.74.8; 9.85.4; 9.85.5; 9.86.27; 9.91.2; 9.97.15; 9.103.1; 9.107.2, 2, 9, 18, 22.)
- The milking cow, kine, is the source of truth, essence, and knowledge.
- Kine are also representative of the union of heaven and earth.

The association of knowledge to cows is deeply ingrained in Vedic thought. The Jaiminiya Brahmana (JB 1.19) makes the following correspondences of cows to knowledge:

- The agnihotra cow is speech.
- The calf of agnihotra cow is mind.
- The milk of the mother cow flows to her calf.
- The milk of agnihotra cow produces the speech that causes the mind to flow.
- This mind of the calf is followed by speech.
- For this reason, the mother cow runs after the calf who walks in front.

In a very stylized manner when it says the mother cow follows the calf the Jaiminiya Brahmana is stating that concepts (the mother cow) precedes the articulation of those concepts in the mind (the calf). Collectively, these correspondences pertain to speech. But even speech is a hidden reference containing a deeper meaning. Speech is the articulation of the world, by attaching a word to an object in the world. For the worshiper to assign the word "tree" to the actual object implies knowledge of that object, albeit through the sense perceptions. This is the hidden meaning of "speech" in the Vedas. Thus considered, the agnihotra cow is that knowledge of the world, and that knowledge is attained through the sacrificial rite. The above portion from the Jaiminiya Brahmana explains the many similes found in the Rg Veda of the mother cow running after or tending to her the calf.

- From RV 1.32.9, which says that after Indra struck while she was tending to her son Danus, Vrtra was above Danu like a cow with her calf.
- From RV 1.38.8, the Marut's lightning roars like a cow for her calf.
- From RV 1.164.9, Heaven (the mother) sustains the Earth (the child), the seed resting in the clouds, the same way the calf bellows for her mother, the cow. This simile emphasizes that the mind is the child of speech.

The correspondence continues:

- The milkpost is the heart.
- The rope is the breath.

With this correspondence the author of the Brahmana makes the following conclusions concerning the relationship of breath, the vital life force, and the mind:

- With the breath the mind and speech are tied to the heart.
- The rope (breath, prana) ties (binds) the cow (speech) and the calf (mind) to the heart.

The cows are an important part of the Vedic dharma. They represent knowledge, wisdom and illumination, most likely because these qualities are representative of their products: milk, butter and ghee. Because the cows produce several by-products, different cows in the Vedas represent different aspects of knowledge or the mind:

- A barren or immature cow is taken to mean the lack of consciousness, incomplete or faulty knowledge, because of its unripe milk. (JB 1.19.)
- The ray-cows represent Aditi, the infinite consciousness. (RV 3.30.14 (unripe milk); 2.7.5; 1.112.3; 1.116.22; 1.117.20; 1.61.9 (raw cows); 6.72.4; 4.19.7; 7.68.8.)
- The Ray-Cows also represent hidden or occult knowledge. (RV 4.58.4; 4.1.6.)
- A cow's calf represents jiva, or the individual soul. (RV 4.33.4; 4.34.5; 1.110.8; 1.111.1; 1.164.5; 1.164.9, 17, 18, 27; 2.7.5; 2.16.8; 2.28.6; 2.24.8; 3.33.3; 3.41.5; 1.55.4; 6.45.25; 5.30.10; 7.87.5; 8.43.17; 8.59.14, 15; 8.61.5; 9.41.14; 9.86.2; 9.100.1,7; 9.104.2; 9.105.2; 9.111.14; 10.8.2, 9; 10.53.11; 10.119.4; 10.145.6; 10.10.75.4;10.123.1.)

Cows are symbolic of a principle or precept of existence:

- Cows follow each other to the sacrifice to find the essence of the Vedic dharma, the Natural Order (*Rta*). (RV 1.53.3.)
- The Cow, knowledge, is associated with *Rta*, the dynamic order of the cosmos. (RV 3.7.2; 1.73.6; 3.7.2; 4.3.9; 4.5.9; 4.23.9; 9.100.7.)
- Cows are a symbol of the potential of creation and sustenance of life. (RV 1.53.5, 6.)
- Cow's milk is representative of that aspect of the Natural Oder, the Vedic dharma (*rta*) the surge of creation. (RV 10.61.19.)
- In a fascinating rc (mantra), the Cows are said to be the light from the unmoving Sun which carries its "six burdens," which is interpreted to mean the six planets of the Vedic solar system. (RV 3.56.2.)
- Cows symbolize the event of cosmic creation, giving to the Vedic dharma (*rta*) by *Rta* alone. (RV 4.23.9.)
- Cows are symbolic of the Word, prayer characterized by beauty, truth and devotion. (RV 8.14.3.)
- Cows symbolize Energy. (RV 3.36.5.)
- Cows symbolize the creation of the universe. (RV 1.164.40, 41; 3.55.1.)

- Cows have the speed of the Rivers Vipas and Sutudi, the waters, or the flow of consciousness. (RV 3.33.1.)
- Cows are compared to light. (RV 1.38.8, 10.)
- Cows are compared to the Waters, the very essence of the Vedic dharma (*rta*). (RV 1.61.10.)
- Cows symbolize the dawn of consciousness or truth. (RV 1.71.1.)
- Cows are symbolic of loyalty. (RV 1.120.8.)
- Cows are associated with the eastern half of the firmament, the mid-world between Heaven and Earth. (RV 1.24.5.)
- Cows are representative of the essence of man. (RV 1.130.5.)
- Cows are symbolic of fullness or plentitude of the Vedic dharma, the Natural Order. (RV 1.135.8.)
- Cows symbolize the seven existential levels of the Vedic dharma. (RV 1.164.3.)
- Cows symbolize the seven rivers. (RV 1.32.12; 2.34.15.)
- Cows symbolize Heaven and earth. (RV 3.6.4; 9.86.2.)
- Cows symbolize Discernment. (RV 2.18.8; 2.38.7.)
- Cows symbolize the powers of knowledge. (RV 3.38.7.)
- Cows symbolize the "seven sisters." (RV 2.7.1.)
- Cows symbolize the provider of nourishment. (RV 3.45.3.) "Nourishment" in the Vedic dharma is spiritual, psychic and material nourishment.
- Cows symbolize Rasa, the quintessence of matter contained in the Vedic dharma. (RV 3.55.16.)

Cows are also symbolic of some aspect of universality, usually in association with other Vedic divine dynamic forces:

- The mother of the Maruts. (RV 5.52.16.)
- As Aditi, the mother of Rudra. (RV 8.101.5.)
- Vrtra's mother lays down like a cow with her calf. (RV 1.32.9.)
- They are compared to or associated with the Maruts. (RV 1.37.5; 1.38.2; 1.85.3.)
- They are compared to or associated with the process of Change (Agni). (RV 1.58.5; 1.66.1; 1.69.2; 4.12.6; 8.43.17.)

- They are compared to or associated with Bala (Indra). (RV 3.41.5; 6.45.25.)
- They are compared to Mother and daughter. (RV 3.55.12.)
- They are compared to the divine Word. (RV 4.12.6.)
- They are the Universal Form and Universal Movement. (RV 4.33.8.)
- They are compared to or associated with Soma, the essence of divine union and religious ecstacy. (RV 9.41.14; 9.69.1; 9.86.2; 9.100.7.)
- They are compared to or associated with the Sindhu Rivers, themselves symbolic of the flow of consciousness. (RV 9.105.2; 9.111.14; 10.75.4.)

The occult meaning of go, the Ray-Cows, consists of two aspects. Go is Vrsabh, the Bull, the Male Principle of Regeneration. (RV 3.38.5.) This principle figured prominently in the eternal law of Creation. Bovine knowledge also holds that go, the cow, also is symbolized in dhenu, the milk-cow, the Female Principle of Creation. (RV 3.38.7.) The Male and Female principles operate together too both creation and supply knowledge of the universe that may be used by the worshiper in the Vedic path to salvation and liberation. The dynamics of these two principles are revealed in 3.38.7. This rc (mantra) states that the Female Principle (dhenu) informs the Male Principle (vrsabh) in the process of creation and regeneration.

- Fire (Agni) is the Male Principle. The Mind is male. (SPB 1.4.4.3.)
- Water (Ap) is the Female Principle. (RV 1.32.11; 1.104.3; 2.35.13; 3.1.7; AB 1.3; SPB, 1.1.1.18, 20; 2.1.1.4; 6.1.1.10; 6.8.2.3.) Speech is female. (SPB 1.4.4.4.)

The union of these polarities are symbolized as the placement of a jug of water near the Garhapatya fire. (SPB 1.1.1.19.) With the Bull and the Milk Cow, that union is represented by Knowledge symbolized in Gonaam. Together, they create a Higher Knowledge which itself creates, dissolves and regenerates the universe. This is the process, Gonaam consists of two processes:

- Vrsabh: Male Principle of Generation.
- Dhenu: Female Principle of Creation.

The Male and Female Principles further and expand the boundaries of knowledge. The Bull, the Male Principle, consists of the following aspects:

- The Bull is Vrsti, signifying Rain.
- The Bull is Vrsan(aa), signifying the Showerer, the Bestower of Benefits.
- The Bull is Vrsabha, signifying the Bull, as related to Purusa.
- The Bull is Vrsaa, signifying the Bull, as the Principle of Regeneration.

Both Indra (Principle of Articulation and Speech)(SA, 5.1, 4) and Agni (Mind)(RV 1.140.2; 1.149.2; 3.1.8; 3.27.13; 3.44.4; 6.16.15; 6.48.3 6; 7.10.1; 8.64.8; 8.93.7, 20; 10.115.2, 8) and Soma (divine mind) are identified as the "Bull" in the Veda. Once milk is boiled during the agnihotra, it is purified and a procreative agent. (MS 1.8.2:117.16 - 19.) As milk is boiled during the agnihotra sacrifice raises, the Male Principle, the Bull, as the Regeneration Principle, implicates and engenders knowledge.

The Milk Cow, dhena, the Female Principle, consists of the following aspects:

- Dhenavah (RV 1.32.2; 1.125.4; 1.135.8; 1.151.5; 2.2.2; 2.5.5; 3.1.7; 4.22.6; 5.6.1, 2; 5.43.1; 5.55.5; 6.45.28; 7.32.22; 9.1.9; 9.13.7; 9.66.6, 12; 9.68.1; 9.77.2; 9.86.17, 25; 9.100.7; 10.32.410.75.4) the "milk cow," cows belong to Indra's manifestation as Conjunction and Unity, and represents the knowledge emanating from Indra after quaffing Soma, Divine Knowledge.
- Dhenavo (RV 1.73.6; 1.84.11; 1.120.8; 1.134.6; 1.135.8; 1.152.6; 1.173.1; 3.7.2; 3.45.3; 3.55.16; 3.57.3, 7; 5.69.2; 7.36.3; 8.70.4; 9.69.4; 9.70.1; 9.97.35; 10.95.6) representing ultimate truth, a high state of knowledge, literally, "full of knowledge."
- Dhenave (RV 8.47.12), representing inspired knowledge.

- Dhenavas (RV 8.4.8), which represents that knowledge which nourishes the worshiper's soul.
- Dhenum (RV 1.20.3; 1.91.20; 1.112.3; 1.118.8; 1.137.3; 1.139.7; 1.160.3; 1.164.26; 2.32.2; 2.34.6; 3.57.1; 4.33.1, 8; 4.34.9; 4.42.10; 5.1.1; 6.35.4; 6.48.11, 13; 6.63.8; 7.18.4; 8.1.10; 10.39.13; 10.61.17; 10.64.12; 10.176.1), or knowledge associated with Soma, or Bliss.

This rc (mantra) makes specific reference to Savitr. As that Vedic principle that dispenses immortality to the other Vedic principles (RV 4.54.2) and forces and salvation and liberation to the mortal Vedic worshiper (RV 1.35.2, 10), the "superior milk" in the rc (mantra) is the highest Knowledge which is the vehicle of liberation and the fruit of the union of the cow and calf.

Energy, consciousness, light, the Waters, the Vedic dharma and the Vedic forces and energies inhabiting and powering the Vedic dharma. These are all bedrock principles in the Natural Order. The Cows have a swath and scope unmatched in the Vedic dharma. The exposition on the Cows continue in the next rc (mantra).

RV 1.164.27:

The cow desires her calf. May the cow give her milk to the Asvins.

A MODEST INTERPRETATION:

Ramamurti distinguishes cows into three groups: The first group consists of go or dhenu, representative of divine, Vedic speech, hymns and prayers. Go and dhenu are also representative of the three levels of the lower world.

Milk, deda, representing, truth, essence, the milk of knowledge. Cows, the primal light, shine on the world. The Asvins, the twin divine principles, represent the principle of Duality. Duality is grounded in the sensible world. The cow, representative of knowledge, informs and sustains the Asvins, by giving milk, the milk of knowledge.

The other group is discussed in the next rc.

RV 1.164.28:

The cow calls out for her calf.
She licks her calf on the forehead, utters a cry and gives it milk.

A MODEST INTERPRETATION:

The cows are also said to produce mantras. (RV 5.45.28; 8.88.1; 8.14.3; 1.25.6; 6.45.7; 9.72.6; 9.84.5; 10.64.12; 2.2.9; 2.34.6; 4.1.15; 4.50.5; 6.45.25; 10.119.4; 9.82.4 (Soma sounding like ray-cows).) The mantras are the sacrificial counterpart of the Word, Logos, the First Principle of the universe. In highly metaphorical language RV 1.164.28 explains that the Logos (First Principle) supports and sustains the sensible world ("her calf") and makes possible for the worshiper to know the sensible world and universe ("licks the calf's forehead"). By "giving milk" the cow ("primal light") extends the reach of its influence.

RV 1.164.29:

The calf bellows as well.
The cow is attached to the calf and cries softly
and mindfully, shining radiantly.

A MODEST INTERPRETATION:

This rc (mantra) speaks of the constant communication exchanged between the sensible world ("calf") and the primal light ("cow"). In that exchange, the Logos ("cow") initially informs and sustains the sensible world, and the world reciprocates to seek, know, and experience the Logos. This communication produces an event discussed in the next rc.

RV 1.164.30:

Life, imbued with breath, moves firm and fast, and rests in the middle.
The Immortal Self, which wanders about at its own volition,
and mortal beings both arise from the same source.

A MODEST INTERPRETATION:

This rc (mantra) discuss a host of issues found in the heart of the Vedic
dharma, the Natural Order (*rta*).

"Imbued with Breath"

This is said many times over the course of Vedic and Hindu literature:
Breath is life and without breath life cannot subsist. Prana is the subtle
aspect of breath. The fire-altar is the sacrificial representation of many
things, including life itself. There is an equivalence between the four
elements of (1) Agni, the Principle of Change and Transformation, (2) the
Earth, (3) the Fire-Altar, and (4) life. (SPB 6.1.1.7, 14; 6.2.2.6; 6.7.1.13;
6.7.3.6; 6.8.2.6, 7.) The Brahmanas note that at every level of the fire-altar,
prana is "something immortal." (SPB 10.1.4.2, 3, 4, 5, 6.) This not only
indicates the sanctity of the fire-altar itself, but points to the underlying
divine nature of the material world.

The Brahmanas concentrate on more mundane matters concerning
how the Agnicayana (the Fire-Altar) is built. There is inner meaning even
in these matters of altar construction. Implicated in the Five-Dimension
Universe, each level of the Agnicayana is constructed with different

elements, impalements and materials. These specifications are hyper-technical. We are not concerned with the composition of the five levels of the Agnicayana, but we are concerned about the result.

- The First Level of the Agnicayana contain ninety-eight elements. (SPB 10.4.3.14.)
- The Second Level of the Agnicayana contain forty-one elements. (SPB 10.4.3.15.)
- The Third Level of the Agnicayana contain seventy-one elements. (SPB 10.4.3.16.)
- The Fourth Level of the Agnicayana contain forty-seven elements. (SPB 10.4.3.17.)
- The Fifth Level of the Agnicayana contain one-hundred and thirty-eight elements. (SPB 10.4.3.18.)

The total number of the elements, impalements and materials used to construct the Agnicayana is three hundred and sixty (360), the days in a year. It is for this reason that the Agnicayana (the Fire-Altar) is said to represent the year. (SPB 10.5.4.10.) Coincidence? Contrived? Perhaps it is no coincidence at all. This is not all the Agnicayana (the Fire-Altar) represents. The Agnicayana (the Fire-Altar) also represents

- The terrestrial, material world. (SPB 10.5.4.1.)
- The air. (SPB 10.5.4.2.)
- The sky. (SPB 10.5.4.3.)
- The Sun. (SPB 10.5.4.4.)
- The Nakshatras. (SPB 10.5.4.5.)
- The Body. (SPB 10.5.4.2.)
- All Beings in the universe. (SPB 10.5.4.12.)

In other words, the Agnicayana (the Fire-Altar) is a microcosm of the Natural Order (*rta*).

"Moves Firm and Fast"

The first stanza of this rc (mantra) demonstrates the Veda's amazing knack at using word play to convey different layers of meaning, one deeper than the other. The three key words at work here are

- Ana, breath.
- Jiva, breath as the underlying principle of life.
- Dhruva, firm and fast, permanent.

According to Monier Williams while both ana and jiva convey breath and breath as the principle of life, only jiva implicates life itself. Both life and breath revolve around dhruva, which according to Monier Williams, means

- Firm and fast, constant, permanent.
- Polaris, the North or Pole Star.
- The sacrificial post onto which the animals/victims were tied.

With dhruva as the nexus of life and the Absolute Self, this rc (mantra) is telling us the following about the Vedic dharma, the Natural Order (*rta*):

- Agni, the Principle of Change and Transformation, is the presiding deity where references to dhruva is mentioned. (RV 1.36; 1.59; 1.73; 1.146; 2.5; 3.6; 4.5; 6.9; 6.15; 10.5.) Change and Transformation is thus the universal constant in the Natural Order.
- Change and Transformation is the eternal law of the Natural Order. (RV 3.6.4; 1.73.3; 2.5.4; 6.9.4; 8.41.9.)
- The principle of Change and Transformation (Agni) is communicated in "the form of light." (RV 6.9.5.)
- This light is diffused as the central point in the Natural Order which empowers all that which moves, and which are stationary. (RV 5.62.1; 10.5.3.)
- This light is centered in the North Star, Polaris, in the Orion constellation. (RV 1.146.1; 8.41.9.)
- Polaris, in turn, becomes the focal point of all events in the sacrifice. (RV 1.36.5; 1.73.3; 1.146.1; 3.54.8; 4.5.4; 8.41.9.)

- The principle of sacrifice thereby becomes another constant in the Natural Order. (RV 1.36.5; 1.73.3; 1.146.1; 6.9.4; 6.15.7.)
- On a ritualistic level the principles of constancy, sacrifice, change and transformation, are channeled in the distillation of Soma Pavamana. (RV 9.20.4; 9.86.6.) It is the very sacrificial rites that celebrate the Natural Order and its principles. The fundamental principles of the Natural Order arrive full circle in the consumption of Soma Pavamana.
- Above all, it is the One, Ekam, which is the lord of the eternal laws which are embedded in the meaning of dhruva. (RV 3.54.8.)

The abode of life (jivam), the material world, however, is to be found at the exchange between ("in the middle") the primal light and the sensible world. The individual Self (jivah), and the mortal body which encases it, have the same source, which is the primal light. This point of exchange, the intermediary region between the world and the light, is referred to in the Vedas as the Svar.

"Rests in the Middle"

The Svar, the shining region of light, was mentioned and discussed in an earlier rc. The Veda indicates that the svar is an intermediate world of heaven and light. (RV 1.35.6.) The emphasis here is a little different. This rc (mantra) says the Svar is located is "in the middle." To discover what this phrase means, and understand that meaning with reference to Vedic cosmology, which is intricate and nuanced, a recap is in order.

Indra as svarajam is the lord and protector of the svar. (RV 1.36.7; 1.51.15; 1.80.1 - 16; 1.84.10, 11, 12; 1.181.2; 2.8.5; 2.28.1; 3.46.1; 3.49.2; 5.58.1; 5.66.6; 5.82.2; 7.66.6; 7.101.5; 8.12.15; 8.61.2; 8.69.17; 8.81.4; 8.93.11; 10.120.8.) As in so many things Vedic, the Vedic dharma operates in terms of triads. The Svar is located above the three levels of earth, the Mid-Earth and heaven, and below the three levels of heavens. There are three subdivisions to each region of heaven and light and each have three subdivisions. Earlier we saw that there were three levels in the Vedic existential hierarchy, with the Svar resting in the middle. As Lord Protector of the Svar, Indra "rest in the middle."

The Svar is something of an enigma. English translations cannot find a common, consistent word to convey the meaning of this word. The English renderings of svar include "Sun," "Sun World," "Light," "Word of Light," "Heaven," "Heaven and Earth," and others. It is all too confusing, which is unfortunate because it conveys an important concept in understanding both the Vedic cosmology and the ultimate arrival point of the soul of the worshiper in the Vedic path to liberation and salvation.

The worshiper's soul passage to heaven is a three-step process. The Svar serves as a way-station, the half-way point prior to arriving at the transcendent heavenly world. The highest heaven is a physical location, the heavens of the sky, whereas the sukrta loka is a subtle, ethereal region of spirit, where the virtuous souls reside. Thus, it is the conduit wherefrom the microcosm is converted to a macrocosmic spirit once it travels through the vortex.

In order to communicate the Svar's function on the both the macrocosmic and microcosmic levels, it is better defined as the "Celestial Region of Immortality." The Svar is sphere where immortality resides. The Svar is that region where light shines eternal. (RV 9.113.7.) To be clear on the nature of the immortality this region houses: Amrta, immortality, is derived from two cognates: "am," according to Monier-Williams, as "going to or towards," and, "serving, honoring." Immortality pertains to and consists of rta, the Vedic dharma. It is the essence of the cosmic order. The svar is the sphere where the pith and marrow of the Vedic dharma is located. This sphere is both a subtle and material region. The Svar is the Center of the Vedic dharma (*rta*). The Vedic divine energies reside in this region where the center of dynamic energies of cosmic order (Svar) is situated. (RV 1.105.3; 4.16.4.) There are noble residents at this Celestial Region of Immortality:

- The dynamic energy present in Indra's manifestation as Bala. (RV 4.23.6.)
- Surya's dynamic energy of the light of knowledge. (RV 10.170.4.)
- The collective Vedic divine energies, the Visvedevas. (RV 1.105.3; 4.16.4; 10.61.14; 10.65.1, 14.)
- The dynamic energy of the light of knowledge (Surya) resides in the region where

- the center of the dynamic energy of the cosmic order (Svar) is situated. (RV 10.170.4.)
- Forefathers residing in the region of the center of the dynamic energy of the Svar. (RV 1.101.3; 5.54.15; 10.14.8; 10.15.4; 10.154.2; AV 18.2.48; PB 9.8.5; TB 1.3.10.5; GB 1.2.4.)

The Vedic heaven is a region where the essence of the dynamic energy of the cosmic order (Svar) participates in and creates the dynamic Vedic energies at work in the cosmic order.

- The principle of change (Agni) is the personification of the region where the center of the dynamic energy of the cosmic order (Svar) is situated. (RV 2.8.4; 7.10.2.)
- The personification of Change is due to its identification with the Water Element RV 1.22.6; 1.122.4; 1.143.1; 1.145.1; 1.186.5; 2.31.6; 2.35.1, 2, 3, 7, 9, 13; 3.9.1; 5.41.10; 6.50.12, 13; 7.34.15; 7.47.2; 10.30.3; 10.92.13; 1.65.3, 4, 9, 10; 1.67.3, 4, 9, 10; 170.3, 4; 1.95.4, 5, 8; 1.44.2; 1.149.4; 2.4.2; 3.1.3; 3.72.2; 3.55.12), an identification shared by the region wherein the center of the dynamic energy of the cosmic order (Svar) is situated. (RV 2.35.6.)
- The energy and dynamism inherent in the principle of change (Agni) creates and sustains the region of the dynamic energy of the Vedic dharma (Svar). (RV 3.2.7.)
- A resident itself in the Water element, Soma, the purified mind and active process of purification, is bathed in light, and generates the region where the essence of the dynamic energy of the Vedic dharma (Svar) is found. (RV 9.86.14.)
- The Svar, the center of the Vedic dharma, is created when the combined energies of Change (Agni) and the process of purification (Soma) slay Vrtra (Ignorance). (RV 10.124.6.)
- The Svar, the center of the Vedic dharma, is sustained with Bala, Indra's manifestation of Might and Energy. (RV 2.21.4; 3.34.8; 5.44.2.)
- The Svar, the center of the Vedic dharma, is created through the combined powers of the collective dynamic Vedic energies (Visvedevas). (RV 10.66.9.)

Underneath the convergence of these energies is the underlying source of the region of the essence of the dynamic energy of the cosmic order (Svar). The flames of the principle of Change (Agni) radiates and commingles in the region of the essence of the dynamic energy of the cosmic order (Svar). (RV 1.59.9; 1.69.10.) The flames fueling the principle of Change (Agni) serves as the glue for all the other energies which converge therein. "In the very beginning the universe was swallowed in darkness. From this darkness the principle of Change (Agni) arose, creating the essence of the dynamic energy of the cosmic order (Svar), and from establishment of the cosmic order from that essence, the dynamic Vedic energies, the earth, heavens, the waters, and all the other forms, arose and delighted on the effluence." (RV 10.88.2.)

It should be noted that RV 10.124.6 describes Agni, in his manifestation as the Principle of Change, as having "seven threads" and Seven-Dimension Universe "five divisions." The "seven threads" refers to the seven levels of Existence and the "five divisions" implicate the Five-Dimensioned Universe inherent in the sacrifice.

The flames of Change (Agni) possess far-reaching implications for the Eternal Laws that guide the worshiper along the Vedic path to liberation. These implications are summarized in the following chart. Each category gives a glimpse of the difference aspects of the principle of Change.

It is indeed an intricate cosmology. Suffice it to say that the Svar is the midway station between the material world and the region of ultimate transcendence. It therefore functions as a vortex to the greater vastness of the three levels of heaven.

We can all obsess on the details of this complicated structure, but that would be a mistake. The most important part of this rc (mantra) is the latter half. That latter half explicitly states that the Immortal Self and mortals originate from the same source. According to this rc, that common source is the Svar, the clearinghouse for heaven. But where did the Svar, where did come from? According to this rc, from the Inner Breath of the Vedic dharma. Where did that Inner Breath come from? According to the previous rc, RV 1.164.29, it originated from the communication exchanged between the sensible world ("calf") and the primal light ("cow"). But what is the essence of that communication? According to RV 1.164.26, and the related rcs which follow, it is Bovine Knowledge, and all that it represents.

The difficulty is that Bovine Knowledge has many aspects. If we had to pick and choose among the many aspects of Bovine Knowledge, and find the essence of that Knowledge, that answer is found in RV 1.164.28, which reveals that the essence of Bovine Knowledge is mantra, which is simply another word for Logos, the Primal Sound, AUM, or any one of its analogous concepts.

Looking back to the Introduction we saw how in ages past the global Zeitgeist was concerned with the Natural Order. That Natural Order was expressed in various ways, the most prominent of which were Logos and our Vedic dharma, *rta*. Here, our Sukta has arrived full circle at this half-way point. It completes its general presentation of *rta*, the Vedic dharma. What follows in the remaining rcs are remaining aspects of the Vedic dharma.

RV 1.164.31:

I beheld Surya, the untiring Protector, traveling
upwards and downwards in his path.
Emitting rays that reach everywhere, they reach the middle.

A MODEST INTERPRETATION:

This rc (mantra) serves many purposes. It returns with a further explanation
of the relationship between Surya and Savitr.

Surya is the Sun and carries a metaphorical meaning of the principle
of Energy and Life. Savitr is associated with Surya and its essence is
embodied in Surya. Their qualities complement each other and together
their interaction oscillates upwards and downwards. From this oscillating
movement energy is generated. The energy generated supplies the basis of
life. It is an awesome phenomenon. Their energy flows to "the middle,"
a reference to the previous rc, where the "middle" is defined as the Svar,
the clearinghouse region of light, Heaven. This is where the rays of Surya
(the Sun) shine, which explains why the Vedas state that Surya bestows
immortality to the gods. (RV 4.54.2.) By the time that immortality
is communicated to the worshiper, it is translated into liberation and
salvation. That power of immortality (liberation and salvation) is contained
in the brilliance of Surya's rays.

RV 1.164.32:

He who has made this state of things, does not know it.
It is hidden from him who see this state of things.
He who is covered in his mother's womb has many offspring
and is born to suffering and evil.

A MODEST INTERPRETATION:

This is an allegory about transmigration and is better understood when considered in reverse order. To be born in this world ("mother's womb") subjects the soul to the endless cycle of death and rebirth ("many offspring") to a world of suffering and evil. Once born, we make the circumstances and choices of our lives, but what do we really know? This rc (mantra) begins the Vedic theme which will be repeated time and again that transmigration and that the true evil in the world is the ignorance associated with this cycle of rebirth.

RV 1.164.33:

The sky is my father; the earth is my mother.
Between them, in the middle, the earth and the sky, held upside down,
and is the source (yoni) of my birth.
The father impregnates the daughter.

A MODEST INTERPRETATION:

It is one thing to be born, or, for that matter, to be reborn. But what is the active principle behind the process of life in the material world? What is the impetus to the creation of life? This rec (mantra) addresses these questions. This rc (mantra) speaks to the conjoining of the Sky and the Earth.

Metaphorically, the rc (mantra) is stating that all life has a divine (Sky) and material (Earth) component

- The Sky, Dyaus, is represented as the Father. (RV 1.52.10.)
- The Earth, Prthvi, is represented as the Mother. (RV 1.52.11.)
- Rodasi, that element of the Natural Order (*rta*) where the Svar is located is that point where they are conjoined. (RV 1.22.13.)

The Svar, rodasi, is the source of my (read, "our, all of us") birth. The impregnation refers to the point of impact of this conjoining. It is a theme which will later be present in the Samkhya philosophy, where the process of evolution begins when Purusa (Sky) makes contact with Prakrti (Earth). Rishi Dirghatama elaborates on this theme in the following rcs.

RV 1.164.34:

I seek the farthest limits of earth.
I wonder where is the inner essence (nahbih) of world.
I seek the semen of a strong horse.
I seek the Word, Logos, the guiding First
Principle which powers the world.

A MODEST INTERPRETATION:

Rishi Dirghatama is setting us up for the operative words found in this rc.
He gives the definitions in the next rc.

RV 1.164.35:

The altar is the farthest limit of the earth.
The sacrifice is the inner essence of the world.
Soma is the semen of the strong horse.

A MODEST INTERPRETATION:

Rishi Dirghatama finally explains the Natural Order (*rta*) in cosmological terms in the context of sacrifice (yajna). In this rc (mantra) sacrifice (yajna) is explained with the following manner in this correspondence:

Farthest limit of Earth	Altar
Inner essence of world	Sacrifice
Seamen of Horse	Soma

"The Altar is the Farthest Limit of the Earth."

The sacrificial altar is the farthest limit of the earth. This modest interpretation has proposed earlier that the sacrificial altar is representative of the Five-Dimension Universe, the gateway to transcendence. This interpretation is confirmed by the Brahmanas. The Satapatha Brahmana goes into great detail concerning the construction of the Agnicayana fire-altar. This explanation contains very intricate and complicated correspondences to the five layers to the Agnicayana fire-altar. While the correspondences themselves are not important to the interpretation of this rc, the hidden meaning of each level is. By identifying the location in the "farthest limit of Earth," the Veda is again speaking in coded language to say that the sacrificial altar encompasses the Natural Order (*rta*) and its contents and inhabitants.

Alluding to the Five-Dimension Universe, the sacrificial altar, especially the Agnicayana, the Fire-Altar, has five levels. According to this explanation, a different Vedic deity presiding over each of the five levels which correspond to a different body part of the worshiper (the microcosm) and carry a different meaning:

Level	Presiding Deity	Corresponding Body Part	Inner Meaning
First	Prajapati	Hair	The in-breath and out-breath
Second	Visvedevas (All Gods)	Skin	Downward breath
Third	Indra, Agni, Visvekarmen	Flesh	Through-breath
Fourth	Rishiis	Bone	Upward breath
Fifth	Parameshthin	Marrow	Central breath

The progression from the lowest of the Agnicayana (the Fire-Altar) to the highest levels correspond to the different levels of prana. Prana is the Vital Principle, the Vital Airs, the life-force which permeates through the cosmos; it is breath of life. The Agnicayana (the Fire-Altar) represents the universe, and this universe is supported by the vital energy of prana. From the lowest level at Samana, where prana peculates upward, to the highest level, where the prana ventilates upwards and downwards, prana is present at every level to nourish and sustain the vitality of the cosmos. The different levels of the Agnicayana (the Fire-Altar) represent different levels and intensity of prana.

The in-breath and out-breath	Prana and Apana
Downward breath	Apana
Through-breath	Vyana
Upward breath	Udana
Central breath	Samana

The Vedic dharma (*rta*) is represented by the Agnicayana (the Fire-Altar). The close association of *rta*, the Vedic dharma, with the sacrificial altar is precisely the reason why Monier Williams defines *"rta"* as "sacrifice." The Agnicayana (the Fire-Altar) also represents the metres uttered in sacrificial chant. (SPB 10.5.4.7.) With this in mind, we segue into the next element in this rc, sacrifice.

"The Sacrifice is the Inner Essence of the World"

The Vedic sacrifice ritual is intended to demonstrate a fundamental truth of the Vedic dharma: That central truth is that there is a give-and-take between the Microcosm (humankind) and the Macrocosm (the universe), and of every object therein, encompassing the process from creation to dissolution. (Sannyasi Gyanshruti, Sunnyasi Srividyananda, *Yajna, A Comprehensive Survey* (2006), pp. 84 – 85.) This give-and-take is the essence of how the Natural Order (Rta) operates. This give-and-take is reflected in the very structure of the Sacrifice.

This give-and-take is an outgrowth of the binary, dualistic Two-Dimensional Universe. On a rudimentary level, this give-and-take is the bargained for exchange for the condition of life in the universe: One being dies so another may live. The dynamics of the exchange takes many forms and is premised on a fundamental assumption that if it is accurately performed sacrifice has a secret power to produce the desired effect. The dynamics in this new level demonstrates the give-and-take process which has been operating every moment in the material universe for eons.

This give-and-take is reflected in many ways. In the sacrificial level, an offering is made to receive blessings. The left-handed movement of the giving is based on a simple premise. Divine powers are associated with and inherent to the action of giving. (RV 1.4.22; TS 1.4.22; VYS 8.2.) The right-handed movement of discernment is reflected in and a product of the sacrifice itself, which establishes consciousness, mind and thought. (VYV 4.19; 4.23; TS 1.2.5.6 - 8.)

This give-and-take is carried out in the simple act of giving of an offering and invoking the divine grace of a deity or God so that the sacrificer may also take his or her desired wish, which is redemption, being born again, purification, or obtain the divinity's grace. In the Soma sacrifice this give-and-take is played out by the "killing" of the Soma plant, the giving its own life literally squeezing its life out through the pressing process, so that the sacrificer receives spiritual benefits in the form of redemption, liberation, and divine bliss.

On an individual level, the essence of yajna, the sacrifice, is the interchange between the embodied soul and conscious human nature and the eternal spirit. It is stated plainly in the Vajaseneyi Yajurveda Samhita that by worshiping Bala (Indra) the worshiper acquires and increases their own Indra-powers (Indriyam), specifically by giving powers of knowledge for the worshipers willing to put forth the effort. (VYS 7.12; RV 5.44.1; 1.4.1; TS 1.49.1.) The dynamics of the give-and-take function of the sacrifice is found in several references:

- As a general proposition the worshiper bestows an offering that the worshiper should accept what the divine dynamic forces give. (VYS 3.50; TS 1.8.4.3.)
- The Vedas also states that in the sacrifice the worshiper kindles the Principle of Change (Agni) that the worshiper may be kindled, and once kindled, kindles the Principle of Change (Agni). (VYS 3.18.)
- The exchange is demonstrated by Food. The worshiper who brings food, receives food. (RV 4.2,7; 4.7.11.)
- This aspect of the give-and-take of sacrifice is stated in the Vajasaneyi Yajurveda Samhita when by worshiping Bala (Indra), those powers inherent in Bala is conveyed to the worshiper. (VYS, 7.12.)

This interchange does not occur without the elimination of the ego-sense. It is only once the ego-sense has been eliminated that the interchange can occur. Without the ego in the way, the human soul may be directed towards the divine. The worshiper therefore coaxes the dynamic forces of the divine with offerings. The offering is the medium of the exchange.

But how is the ego-sense eliminated? According to this rc, only with the medium of divine madness. That madness, those means to "get out of our minds" is through the final element of this rc (mantra), Soma.

"Soma is the Semen of the Strong Horse"

The first level of the altar is the highest, the closest level to heaven. This is where Prajapati resides. This is the level represented by the Soma sacrifice. (SPB 10.1.5.3.)

Soma takes several forms. Among others, Soma is a Vedic force and principle and it is a sacrificial substance. Here, Soma is called the "semen of the horse." Applying what we have learned from Equine Knowledge, this rc (mantra) says Soma acts upon the senses. That it is the "semen" of the horse, this is coded language that Soma is the inner essence of and gives birth to this knowledge. Soma is thus characterized as the inner essence of the senses.

This rc (mantra) ends inwards in the deepest levels of the human psyche. The next rc (mantra) changes perspective upwards to the farthest reaches of the Vedic dharma (order).

RV 1.164.36:

Seven half-seeds, the inner essence of the world,
perform their functions
according to the command of Vishnu.
With their thoughts they pervade and encompass all the universe.

A MODEST INTERPRETATION:

Vishnu is the Lord of protection, sustenance & maintenance of the world. Seven is a number imbued with holy, divine implications. We saw earlier the role Seven played in the Vedic dharma. This rc (mantra) gives us the most important function of the number Seven.

"The Seven Half-seeds"

The seven half-seeds are the seven laws which in turn protect, sustain, and maintain the world. These laws are eternal and pervade the universe.

The Vedas reflect the revelation of Eternal Laws. The philosophy of the Rg Veda can be reduced to seven Eternal Laws. The Eternal Law of *Rta*, the focus of the Asyavamasya Sukta, is only one of these seven laws. The Vedas in general and the Rg Veda have for millennia been said to possess these Eternal Laws of the universe. These laws have their own internal principles and attributes from which these Eternal Laws operate and inhere in the principle divinities which are the subjects of this book: Agni, the Principle of Change; Indra, the principle of Knowledge and Divine Grace; and Soma, the Principle of Purification and Divine Union.

These principles all possess attributes, which are characteristics shared between these principles/divinities and find expression in the suktas and rcs of the Rg Veda, the mantras of the Yajur Veda, and the samans of the Samaveda. It is these Eternal Laws, principles and attributes hold the secret to understanding the Rg Veda and are the subjects of this books.

These Eternal Laws are responsible for the creation, operation, dissolution, and subsequent re-creation of the universe and everything within. Agni, Indra, and Soma each play its own role in maintaining the universe; indeed, they, or more precisely, the Eternal Laws they represent, are the major framers of the universe and its maintenance. Some, if not most, of those Eternal Laws are hardly surprising considering further developments in Indian thought, as these Eternal Laws would constitute the core of what the Western world calls "Hinduism." These Eternal Laws have their origin in the suktas and rcs of the Rg Veda, the yajurs of the Yajurveda, the samans of the Sama Veda, and the mantras of the Brahmanas, and originate from other ancient Vedic writings. The Seven Laws are a template within which the Vedic forces rule and govern *rta*, the Natural Order. There are seven laws testify to the transcendent truth of the Vedas.

The seven Eternal Laws are:

- One, the Eternal Law of Creation.

  Creation is a single, cyclical, event. Vedic creation is without a "beginning" or an "end." But there are four aspects of Vedic creation. All aspects are found in the Tenth Mandala. If a "beginning" must be posited it is described in RV 10.129, in which a state of indiscriminateness is described, a place where there is neither existence nor non-existence and darkness envelopes darkness. From there, RV 10.121 describes the hiranyagarbha, the cosmic seed from where the multiplicity of the world developed. RV 10.90 describes the Purusa, the embodiment of the Macrocosmic Person. RV 10.190 establishes *rta*, the cosmic law regulating the order of the universe, as well as its subsidiaries Satya and dharma. Finally, RV 10.130 establishes the cosmic ramifications of sacrifice.
- Two, the Eternal Law of the One.

Ekam, the One, is self-created and appeared early in the scheme of creation, in the first stage found in RV 10.129. It will be repeated several times in this book that while the number of divinities in the Vedas are legion they are all manifestations of the One God. There is in fact only one God, and It is referred to principally as Ekam, "the One." The divinities each have their own characteristics. Agni, for instance, is commonly known as the God of Fire, but as interpreted in this book is typified by the Eternal Law of Change which is possessed of several attributes explained in this book. The characteristic of Fire, is shared among other divinities. This only emphasizes the unity of God. The underlying unity of the divinities is shared with phenomenal manifestation. So, while there is an underlying unity in the divinities, that unity is shared with the phenomenal universe, both and between that of the divine.

- Three, the Eternal Law of *Rta*.

    Rta is the cosmic dynamic order in the universe, the Vedic dharma. The Veda may be seen as a panegyric to *rta*, the dynamic Vedic forces subject to the dictates of this dynamic order, yet, in true Vedic manner, at the same time its overlords. It is the task of the worshiper to find its place in this dynamic order while traversing on the Vedic path to liberation and salvation.

- Four, the Eternal Law of Consciousness.

    Once God established the universe and created the internal mechanism for its regulation, the Eternal Law of consciousness arose. The Eternal Laws which inhere in Agni and Indra each provide their own particular role in the establishment and maintenance of consciousness.

- Five, the Eternal Law of Sacrifice.

    The preceding Eternal Laws pertain primarily to the worshiper and the worshiper's place in the material universal. The Eternal Law of Sacrifice, while a present at the creation of the material universe, serves a double purpose in symbolizing the mechanism by which the creation operates and providing that same mechanism by which the soul of the worshiper is elevated. That mechanism is found in the give-and-take interchange which is the essence of sacrifice. It is through this give-and-take mechanism that the worshiper arrives at the Eternal Laws which follow.

- Six, the Eternal Law of Knowledge.

     Vedanta was concerned first and foremost to how knowledge is obtained. This is not the concern of the Vedas. Knowledge is revealed, and while communicated through the Rishis, always had and always will exist. There are different forms of knowledge, and it is part of the worshiper's task in the path to liberation and salvation to discover and implement that knowledge. This is the area to which the Eternal Law of Knowledge is concerned.

- Seven, the Eternal Laws of Salvation and Liberation.

     One difficulty is identifying separate laws. The philosophy of the Rg Veda is very much an organic whole. One Eternal Law refers to another and each refer to the others. The number of the Eternal Laws were fixed at seven essentially as an arbitrary number, yet appropriate given the significance the Vedas attach to the number seven.

The seven-half seeds could also be interpreted to mean the Seven-Dimensional Universe or the seven levels of existence or any of the other applications discussed in an earlier rc (mantra).

RV 1.164.37:

I did not understand this all and roamed aimlessly in hiding
attempting to understand this.
Then the first born of *Rta* consisting of its laws came to me
and I began to understand the Word
and participate in the speech.

A MODEST INTERPRETATION:

The Asyavamasya is getting ahead of itself. To understand this rc (mantra) the distinction between the Word and Speech should first be explained. This distinction is fully discussed later in RV 1.164.45.

While *Rta* is only one of the seven eternal laws which rule creation, and guide the worshiper in the path to liberation, it has special significance. In one sense, the quest for liberation and salvation is the desire to understand the cosmic force which pervades everything. Once understood, the worshiper begins to understand the basis of how creation is articulated, here signified by the Word, and how the phenomena in that creation assumes form. The articulation is not limited to form, but once the cosmic laws are understood, the worshiper is able to communicate that import to others.

RV 1.164.38:

With up and down movements, I become immortal through
svadha, even though I remain a mortal person.
These up and down movements are eternal movements and go in
different directions. They understand, yet do not understand, each other.

A MODEST INTERPRETATION:

Svadha is the process by which the worshiper implements the values
inherent in the Vedic divine energies into everyday practice. Through
the application of values into everyday use the worshiper achieves
liberation and salvation, rendered in this rc (mantra) as "immortality."
This application is achieved through meditation, here described as an up-
and-down movement, a version of the give-and-take process discussed in
RV 1.164.35. Understanding is not attained when the mind wanders in
all directions. When focused and concentrated, the mind ("they") is in a
better position to practice svadha ("understands").

RV 1.164.39:

The gods sit and take their supreme position
on hearing the rcs of the Veda.
What can a person do if they do not know this?
Those that do understand the rcs sit with the gods.

A MODEST INTERPRETATION:

RV 1.164.29 essentially summarizes the previous rc. When the values and principles of the Vedic divine energies are internally implemented the worshiper is liberated and saved. This rc (mantra) contemplates that the worshiper "sits with the gods," i.e., is liberated and is saved, upon understanding the import of the Veda.

Exactly where does the worshiper "sit"? The Sanskrit text calls this area the *parama vyoma*. This is a lofty position, but is it above the Seven or even Five Dimension universe? The answer is Yes and No. This is a space of like no other, but the word "space" may be misleading, because that word implies a physical location and mass. It is what this modest interpretation calls The Land of Pure Being, a region beyond any physical, material presence.

Turiya is the Land of Pure Being. It is that transcendental realm beyond the beyond and inherently different than the physical universe. The region of Pure Being is above the entire cosmological scheme. According to the Three-Dimensional Universe there are three divisions to the upper three worlds of the unmanifested region of pure Being. Commentators disagree as to the nomenclature of these three subdivisions. The names of these subdivisions have been identified as parama vyoma (RV 162.7; 1.143.2; 1.164.34, 35, 39, 41; 3.32.10; 4.50.4; 5.15.4; 5.63.1; 6.82; 7.5.7; 7.82.2; 9.85.12; 10.5.7; 10.14.8; 10.123.5; 10.129.7), ekam sat (RV 1.164.46), and para, but also identified as priya (or maya), urja, and vasu. The upper three regions of Pure Being has also sometimes been referred to as paravaata (RV 1.32.10; 1.36.18; 1.39.1; 1.48.7; 1.73.6; 1.92.3; 1.128.2; 3.37.11; 3.40.8, 9; 4.26.6; 5.53.8; 5.61.1; 6.8.5; 6.44.15; 6.45.1; 7.97.2; 8.3.17; 8.5.20; 8.7.26; 8.12.6; 8.30.3; 8.32.22;9.68.6; 10.95.14; 10.137.2; 10.144.4; 10.145.4; 10.180.2; 10.187.2) or simply para, "beyond." These are all synonyms in the Rg Veda for this highest existential region known as Pure Being.

The rishis of the Vedas were all familiar with the transitoriness of the material world. They saw higher, truer worlds. The three stages creation following the Nadisya Skukta very much represents the transitory, transmigratory world of birth and rebirth, which, on an existential level, is the life condemned for those who have not achieved liberation or who have aspired to higher sentential levels of consciousness. The place described by the Nadisya Sukta is the indeterminate state which is variously viewed as the place of mystic union with god or that level of divine existence. Just as the Vedic divinities are different manifestation of the Single One, there are many names for the region of Pure Being.

The region of Pure Being is also described as mahiih (RV 1.140.5; 2.15.5; 3.33.8; 2.34.8; 4.19.6;4.32.7; 5.43.6; 5.44.6; 5.85.5, 6; 9.41.6; 9.65.1), because it conveys the vastness of Pure Being, although mahiih is also used to convey might, strength, and vigor, usually in connection with Indra. Pure Being is both a physical place and psychological state. As a psychological state it is that level of Pure Being where the Paratman and ultimate Self-Realization dwells. As we saw, the Veda has many expressions for this State of Pure Being. One such expression is parame vyoma.

As a physical place, parame vyoma means, literally, "the highest place." As the highest place it is not simply the highest level of the cosmological realm, but a place set apart from the other levels of existence because of its inherent qualities, where, according to the Nasadiya Sukta, existence and non-existence exists. It is also the birthplace of the divinities. It is the place of origin where all the principles inherent in the divinities reside (RV 1.164.39). It is here that the Vedic forces of Indra and Transformation (Agni) were born. (RV 3.32.10.) It is where the very source of Deification and Divination (Soma) dwells with the power of Divine Grace (Indra). (RV 9.86.15.)

Parame Vyoma is also a psychological state. It is made a psychological state through the agency of selected Vedic forces. The principle of Transformation (Agni), as soon as it appeared in the realm of Pure Being (parame vyoma), placed the spark of consciousness in the firmament. (RV 6.8.2.) Brhaspati, as soon as it appeared in this region, created the seven layers of consciousness and the entire multitude of physical forms. (RV 4.50.4.)

These divine qualities and others are crystallized in the place of the sacrificial alter (RV 5.15.2), where, once reborn, the worshiper is united with this highest place of Pure Being. (RV 1.143.2.)

The Vedic force (deity) representing this highest state of Pure Being is Brhaspati. Brhaspati is the Supreme manifestation of consciousness. The appellation literally means "Lord of the Vast (the psychological state of Pure Being)."

RV 1.164.40:

May you be happy eating the barley grass.
The cow will not be harmed and allowed to eat the grass,
drink the water and wander about.

A MODEST INTERPRETATION:

This rc (mantra) sets us up a new round of discussion which will proceed
for the next group of stanzas

"The Barley Grass"

Barley grass was widely used in sacrificial rites and serves many
purposes to represent various aspects of the Natural Order. Barley grass
represents

- Fire, the medium of change, and Agni, the Principle of Change
  (TS 6.6.3.3; 6.4.3.3; SPB 12.4.3.1; 3.9.3.1; ASSu 8.7.28; KS
  29.3.171.5), and Expiation, redemption, forgiveness. (SPB 3.9.4.17.)

Representing the inner seat (of grass) wherein the vision of Agni
Pavamana is made, Barhi is a manifestation of the terrestrial Fire of Agni.
In a sacrificial setting the Barhi is the seat of grass whereupon sits the
worshiper, the supplicant, the visiting Vedic forces and energies from which
the worshipers and supplicants seek divine inspiration. The terrestrial fire
of Barhi is more than simply the grass circling the Sacrificial Fire:

- Barhi is subsumed in Narasamsa, itself a manifestation of the terrestrial Fire of Agni. (BD 1.107.) Nara is the Primeval Man, the Purusa, Manu, Adam in the Abrahamic religions, an. Nara is also the Universal Spirit pervading the Universe. The terrestrial fire of Narasamsa is the most excellent, most exalted, manifestation of Nara. Given this equivalence, in a very macrocosmic manner, the terrestrial fire of Barhi has cosmic implications. Yet, because it is a terrestrial fire, it also has implications to the material world.
- On a personal level, the terrestrial fire is born from the personal self-surrender of the worshiper. In this regard, the Veda states that the terrestrial fire of Barhi is made from the worshiper's self-surrender. (RV 6.11.5.) On a physical level, the Barhi grass resembles foliage. On a mystic level, when the worshiper surrenders totally to the Sacrificial Fire, the heat merges to be conveyed and communicated to the seat of Barhi grass.

The most prominent of the Vedic invitees is the Vedic force of Agni. Agni arrives in his many capacities:

- The Vedic force of Agni arrives as the Messenger, summoning the other Vedic forces and energies. (RV 1.12.4.)
- As the Messenger, the Vedic force of Agni asks the other Vedic forces and energies to sit on the middle of the Barhi. (RV 3.13.1.)
- At the same token, the gods invite Agni to sit on the Barhi grass. (RV 3.9.9.)
- Most times, the Vedic force of Agni sits on the Barhi simply to complement the presence of the forces of the Vedic dharma. (RV 5.26.5; 7.11.2; 8.44.14.)
- Consistent with his capacity as the summoning Vedic force, the Vedic force of Agni sits on the Barhi as the hotra, the reciter of invocations and litanies. (RV 6.16.10.)
- The Vedic force of Agni occasionally acts as a "middle man" and sits on the Barhi alone, sending oblations, offerings, thoughts, prayers, supplications, to the other Vedic forces and energies. (RV 4.9.1; 8.23.26.)

- Agni in his capacity as the unifier of Heaven and Earth. (RV 1.144.6.)
- When the Vedic force of Agni arrives at the Sacrifice, the worshiper experiences Bliss and contentment. (RV 7.11.2.)

"The Cow Will Not Be Harmed"

Barley grass also represents protection:

- Barley grass is used as a buffer to the spade while constructing the sacrificial altar, least the earth be harmed. (KS 2.6.15; SPB1.2.4.15; ASSu 2.1.5.)
- A blade of barley grass is placed on the victim for protection before it is sacrificed. (KS 6.6.8; SPB 3.8.2.12.)

And so is the cow protected here in this rc, allowed to drink the water and wander about while it is eating the grass. The Cow is further explained in the next rc (mantra).

RV 1.164.41:

The ruddy cow utters the luminous word and makes a sound.
This word speaks in a one-footed, two-footed, four-footed, eight-
footed, and nine-footed phrases, in thousands of letters.

A MODEST INTERPRETATION:

This rc (mantra) expands on the meaning of the Cow. The Cow is representative of the mantra, the Word, logos. This rc (mantra) also in speech. It is also about color and how color fits in the Vedic dharma. Color introduces us to the role of alchemy in the Vedic dharma.

"The Ruddy Cow," the Luminous Word"

A ruddy cow is not your average cow. English translators of H.H. Wilson and Griffith do not give this cow a color, but this rc (mantra) does. But what about the color, "Ruddy"? Ruddy is defined as a "blood red." It also talks about the "luminous word." Luminous is bright, golden. And what is the significance of this color in the Natural Order? Like colors on the spectrum, a relationship exists with blood red and gold.

Color graces the visible Natural Order. The material world is bathed with color. For instance, there is gold. Gold is the most prominent color and the color most pregnant with meaning. Gold is a metal, but it is also a color. Gold is the true color of the Sun, not orange which is the result of pollution, both naturally occurring and man-made. Therefore, it is natural that Savitr is associated with gold:

- Savitr is golden-eyed. (RV 1.35.8.)
- Savitr is golden-handed. (RV 1.35.9, 10.)
- Savitr is golden-tongued. (RV 6.71.3.)
- Savitr has golden arms. (RV 6.71.1, 5; 7.71.1; 7.45.2.)
- Savitr is golden haired. (RV 10.139.1.)
- Savitr wears a tawny, golden-hued garment. (RV 4.53.2.)
- Savitr drives a golden car with a golden pole. (RV 1.35.2, 5.)
- With his strong golden arms, he blesses all creatures. (SPB 2.38.2; 4.14.2; 6.71.1, 5; 7.45.3.)

The references to gold harkens to the color of sunlight, but also to the properties of the metal. The ancients held gold in high esteem because the metal itself does not tarnish or rust. Aside from its shiny color, these properties give gold and all things golden the metallic equivalent of the eternal, which is undying, immortality and unborn. (MS 2.2.2; KS 21.6.44.4; SPB 2.2.2.1; 4.3.4.28; 4.5.2.10; 4.6.1.8, 6; 5.2.1.20; 5.4.1.14; 6.7.2.2; 7.4.2.17; AB 2.14.) Gold, the metal and the color, is the attribute of Savitr, the giver of life. Gold represents the essential qualities of life:

- Light, the substratum of life. (SPB 6.7.2.1, 2.)
- Prana, the Vital-Life Principle. (SPB 6.7.1.11; 6.7.2.1, 2; 7.4.1.16, 17; 7.4.2.8; 8.1.4.1; 12.5.2.6.)
- The Vital Energy of the universe. (SPB 3.3.37; 5.4.1.13; 6.7.1.4, 9; 6.7.4.2; 12.9.1.4.)

Gold is highly symbolic of the attributes of immortality, aptly summarized in the Pacavimsa Brahmana:

- Mahas, the personification of strength and greatness. (PB 18.7.6.)
- Prakasa, the light of consciousness. (PB 18.7.7; ASS 18.2.11.)
- The light infused to the worshiper's soul. (PB 18.7.8.)
- The world of heaven. (PB 18.7.9, 10.)

Gold is the defining characteristic of Agni, the Principle of Change and Transformation.

- Fire, the principal characteristic of Agni, in his manifestation of the Principle of Change and Transformation, is equated with Gold. (SPB 13.4.1.7.)
- Gold is known as the "seed of Agni." (SPB 2.1.1.5; 2.2.2.28; 2.2.4.15; 3.2.2.2; 3.3.13; 3.2.4.8; 3.9.4.1; 4.5.1.15; 5.2.3.6; 5.3.1.1; 5.5.1.8; 14.1.3.14, 29.)

How is Gold the "seed of Agni"? The very nature of Color has something to do with this meaning. The brilliance of gold the metal is similar to the brilliance of fire. But as the metal gold is very malleable, it can change form without losing any efficacy in its powers. In this respect, gold is the perfect metaphor for Agni as the Principle of Change and Transformation. Just as Gold is freely changeable, Agni's capacity for change and transformation effortlessly changes form yet retains its underlying substance and efficacy. This underlying characteristic of Agni pervades the Vedic dharma, the Natural Order. The underlying substance of the Natural Order will not change, different wine but same bottle, if you will, but retains its power. This is the ultimate paradox of the Vedic dharma: Stability based on constant change and transformation. This is the "luminous word."

What about the "ruddy cow"? The foregoing is relevant because gold, the metal and the color, is at the top of coloring hierarchy of existence. Much later this rc (mantra) and other passages from the Vedas will much later serve as the inspiration for the alchemical arts. The underlying basis of alchemy had its origins in the Vedas, and the Rg Veda may be interpreted as an alchemical text. The ultimate purpose of alchemy is the search for the Philosopher's Stone. There is a similar color chain in the alchemical process which transmutes base materials into the rasa (Elixir). The rasa is a result of the transmutation of mercury into gold. It is an elixir capable of curative powers for both physical and spiritual ailments. This alchemical process involves many preparatory steps. (R., 34 - 151.) Once these steps are completed, however, the ayurvedic doctor will produce a paste (bhasmas) of various colors:

- First the doctor will produce a yellow paste. (R, 152.)

- After further processes, the good doctor will produce a red paste. (R., 156.)
- This red paste is a Sulphur which is thereafter processed into gold. (R., 157.)

The "Ruddy Cow," then, represents that level of understanding not enlightened enough to be called "Gold," but awakened enough to have been freed, however fleetingly, from the chains of ignorance. It is a middling spiritual state, a spiritual journey just begun and continuing towards liberation and salvation. The gold produced is not intended to mean material wealth. The purpose of this processed gold is to produce deha siddhi, an immortal body. (R., 202.) This purpose is echoed in treatise after alchemical treatise. Thus, just as the red-colored bhasma signifies the penultimate step in the process to arrive at the golden elixir, so in the Veda, the color red, as applied to the ruddy cows, is said to represent the onset or beginnings of illumination and/or knowledge. (RV 1.92.2; 10.68.6; 6.64.3; 1.49.1; 8.7.7.) This, then, is the meaning of this stanza. The ruddy cow represents that stage just prior to illumination.

The word uttered by the Cow is "luminous," golden. Since this word is golden it implicates the ultimate truth of the universe. But how can that ultimate truth be uttered with the limitations of gross speech and articulation? The answer is that the ultimate truth cannot be spoken. It is essentially unknowable. The mantra of the ruddy cow is the highest form of true speech given the limitations of the material world. The next rc (mantra) further elaborates on this theme.

RV 1.164.42:

The ocean flows from this ruddy cow and flows in the four directions.
The whole of existence flows from that ocean.

A MODEST INTERPRETATION:

The ocean is symbolic of the universal Atman, the vast reservoir of
Consciousness. (RV 1.8.7; 1.11.1; 1.19.7; 1.32.2; 1.52.4; 1.71.7; 1.95.3;
1.110.1; 1.116.4; 1.117.15; 1.130.5; 1.167.2; 1.173.8; 1.174.9; 1.190.7;
12.19.3; 3.33.2; 3.36.6; 3.46.4; 4.55.6; 5.44.9; 5.85.6; 6.17.12; 6.20.12;
6.30.4; 6.36.3; 6.50.14; 6.69.6; 7.33.8; 7.35.13; 7.49.1; 7.69.7; 7.88.3; 8.3.4;
8.3.10; 8.6.13, 25, 35; 8.12.2, 5; 8.34.13; 8.92.22; 8.97.5; 8.102.4, 5,
6; 9.12.6; 8.29.3; 9.61.15; 9.63.23; 9.64.8; 9.64.16, 17, 19. 27; 9.73.3;
9.84.4; 9.85.10; 9.86.6; 9.88.6; 9.96.19; 9.91.40; 9.107.9, 14, 15, 23;
9.108.16; 9.109.4; 10.30.3; 10.58.5; 10.66.11; 10.72.7; 10.89.11; 10.98.5;
10.114.4; 10.121.4; 10.123.8; 10.142.7, 8; 10.143.5; 10.149.1, 2, 3.) The
four directions are symbolic of the entire universe which pervades creation.
The whole of existence flows from the universal atman. The Cow in this
rc (mantra) represents Vak, the Articulation of Mind and Matter (Logos).
That articulation is reflected in the letters of the alphabet, which in later
matrika traditions, in the Tantra, would acquire mystic qualities traditions
to define the world, "in the four directions."

RV 1.164.43:

I see the smoke rising from the cow-dung.
The heros have cooked the spotted bull.
They become the first dharmas.

A MODEST INTERPRETATION:

There are two possible interpretations to this rc. On one level, based on external yajna principles, it reflects the cooking of the sacrificial bull. On the other, deeper, level, based on internal yajna, it is the prior, unenlightened, life of the worshiper who is sacrificed. As the previous life passes, the remnants of that life raise higher to heaven.

There is another dimension. Smoke has repeatedly been a metaphor in Indian logic for inference. When smoke is seen this is an inference there exist a fire. "Where there is smoke there is fire." The inference of fire becomes important when attempting to prove the existence of god. So as the argument goes, just as fire exists when smoke is seen, so God exists because His product, i.e., the world, exists. For this reason, the heroes who cook the spotted bull, become the first dharma. These heros are the First Cause of the creation.

RV 1.163.44:

The three look down on the seasons of the earth.
One shears the ground; another gazes upon the entire universe.
The other's motion is seen but form is not.

A MODEST INTERPRETATION:

Rishi Dirghatama returns to speak of the Principle of Change (Agni), Energy (Surya), and the Principle of Effulgence. The Principle of Change (Agni) is the process of purification and dissolution. By shearing, burning, the ground, creation is reduced to their basic element. Energy (Surya) is the power source of transformation. Principle of Effulgence is the vital force of evolution powered by Surya. These three energies rule creation. This rc (mantra) later evolved to the doctrine of trimurti, and the three energies of the Principle of Change (Agni), Energy (Surya), and the Principle of Effulgence later fulfilled the functions of Brahma, Vishnu and Siva, to create maintain and dissolve the universe.

We learned more about the one face of the Sun, Savitr, a few rcs (mantras) ago. This rc (mantra) mentions the other aspect of the Sun, Surya. Observing the shining orb of the Sun, Surya is likened to an "eye," which makes perfect sense because both are round:

- Surya is eye of Agni. (RV 1.115.1.)
- Surya is the eye of Mitra and Varuna. (RV 6.51.1; 7.61.1; 7.63.1; YV 4.35; 7.42; 13.46; AV 13.2.35.)

- Surya is the eye of Usas, the Dawn, the Vedic dynamic force representing mental awareness. (RV 7.77.3.)
- Surya is the "lord of the eyes." (AV 5.24.9.)

The next rc (mantra) changes gears into an entirely different subject. Speech.

RV 1.164.45:

Speech is divided into four parts.
Three of those parts are occult and subtle.
The last part is uttered by people.

A MODEST INTERPRETATION:

This rc (mantra) begins a tradition later firmly established and repeated and expanded time again in Vedic doctrine. According to that tradition, there are four levels of articulation of the names of forms in creation, each level evolving into the other.

- Vaikhari is the spoken word, the gross aspect of articulated speech.
- Madhyama consists of a mix of subtle and gross states. The subtle state consists of the seven primary notes. These are the seven notes of the saman chant. Externally these are the notes chanted during the sacrifice; esoterically these notes are the rhythm and vibration of the universe.
- Pasyanti, which is the all-perceiving state of Brahman full of energy.
- Para, is the paratman, Logos, the Word, entirely subtle and intangible.

While this is nominally concerning the levels of speech, on a deeper level this pertains to the levels of reality, from the gross material level, to the spiritual level of the Atman, and beyond the Atman. The process begins with articulated speech, such as one person to another, and raises to the level of abstraction where, depending on the particular school of Hinduism, it is called bindu, parabindu, nada, or AUM — all of which are manifestations of the primal sound emitted at the beginning of creation. It is there, at the beginning of creation, that this primal sound resides.

- Vaikhari is the spoken word of one person to another.
- Madhyama is the spoken word as understood and interpreted in the mind from one speaker to another. This is a subtle, unspoken process.
- Pasyanti is meaning of the word from an etymological or historical perspective. This too is a subtle, unspoken process.
- Para, is the inner meaning of the word which exists independent from human understanding, the Logos, residing as a Platonic form, the noumenon, the paratman, the esoteric meaning of all Word. This is the most subtle level of all.

This classification has been repeated countless times over the course of Vedic and Hindu thought.

The Word is represented in the sacrifice by the sacrificial chant. (RV 1.182.4; 4.57.5; VS 17.57; av 3.20.10; 4.6.2.) Sama is a type of chanting reserved especially for the Soma sacrifice, and one of the Vedas, the SamaVeda, is devoted entirely to those chants recited during the Soma sacrifice. As we saw, there are two aspects to Saman.

- The material meaning of the word is associated with the practice of yajna.
- The esoteric meaning of saman, developed more fully in later Vedas, is "vital force" a forerunner to "prana," and the cause of creation itself. On a deeper level the esoteric meaning of saman is a correspondence of the expanding and contracting movements of the universe, on the micro- and macrocosmic levels.

The sequential aspects of *Rta* establishes the vibration in the cosmos which regulate all things. The sequential aspects of sama translates that vibration into the rhythms and cadences of the hymns at the sacrifice. The sequential aspects of both are reflected in the oscillations between the left and right-handed movements. The expansion/contraction movements of sama represent the left and right-hand movements of the cosmic order.

RV 1.164.46:

They speak of Indra, Mitra, Varuna (Lord
Protector of the Vedic dharma),
and fire (Agni). The learned speak of many names, but there is only one.
The one is a winged bird.

I have tendered three twigs
But their branches and stalks are bound to another:
"They come forth together but have different names,"
As they all stem from one gate.

Cantong qi: 3.23 - 26.
The Seal of the Unity of Three,
Pregadio, trans.

A MODEST INTERPRETATION:

If anyone knows anything about the Asyavamasya Sukta, it is this rc
(mantra). It is probably the best summarization of the philosophy of the
Rg Veda. It extols unity and tolerance. This rc (mantra) is the essence of
the Asyavamasya Sukta. Indeed, it is the essence of Vedic thought and
sensibilities in general. All divine Vedic energies are the manifestations of
the one God. Here, the bird emphasizes the ethereal nature of God. Most
frequently cited to state the ultimate unity of the dynamic Vedic forces,
the essence of this rc (mantra) is articulated in the AtharvaVeda, with a
twist. In AV 9.10.28, similar, if not identical, language is spoken to relate

that the Rishiis speak of the One reality, ekam sat, but that "these thinkers speak in speculation."

The Rg Veda says the One is the product of the synergy of three primal Vedic forces which arose from the vast primeval indiscriminate mass (asat):

- *Rta*, which has a luminous nature,
- Satya, which has a luminous nature, and
- Tapas, which is the creative heat of Pure Energy. (JB 3.360.)

We haven't quite yet arrived at the appearance of shape and form. For now, that the One has been created, in the vast cosmological scheme of the Rg Veda, consciousness, is created. The One brings forth the individual forces of which Consciousness consists (RV 10.129.4):

- Kama (desire);
- The seed (retas) of Mind (Manas);
- Hrd, the Heart;
- Pratiishya, purposeful impulse, and
- Thought (Manisha).

Predating by millennia what we now know about the structure of the universe, the Veda says that what we commonly call "matter," contains at its core anti-matter, or asat, the same substance from which shape and form arise. (RV 10.129.4.) This is the ultimate paradox of the physical existence.

The paradoxes do not stop there. Also at the heart of the macrocosm lies the divine. This rc (mantra) addresses a common concern of the uninitiated. How can Hinduism recognize so many gods, when there is but one God? There is indeed but one God, but the many Hindu deities are the different manifestations of the one God, each having their own capability, power and influence. The One is therefore the Many and the Many is the One.

The deities indeed are forces, principles, and powers which fuel the Natural Order (*rta*). In summary

- Surya, the Vedic force and principle embodying Energy.

- Agni, the Vedic force embodying the principle of Change or Transformation.
- Ghrta, or ghee, the Vedic attribute incorporating the quality of Effulgence or Illumination.
- Brhaspati, the Vedic force embodying the principle of the Supreme manifestation of consciousness.
- The Asvins, Vedic forces which serve many purposes, but which generally represent that aspect of Duality in motion.

The list goes on. A more complete list is in the Appendix. For now, Rishi Dirghatama changes gears once again to explore another aspect of the Vedic dharma (*rta*)

RV 1.164.47:

The ruddy birds raise to heaven on the dark path, clothed in the waters.
The birds return from the realm of the divine cosmic order.
When they arrive, the surface of the world is blanketed with ghee.

A MODEST INTERPRETATION:

In the first rc (mantra) Ghee is the second brother established in the Vedic equation establishing the Natural Order (*rta*). As far as the Asyavamasya Sukta is concerned, birds generally represent the universal Atman. That the Rishii calls these "ruddy birds" signify a soul which has not yet received self-realization. They fly along a "dark path," meaning one which is not illuminated, but they are "clothed in the waters." In the Vedas, "water" is metaphorical for purification. Purified, the soul arrives to heaven. The waters purify the birds (the soul), and, like the man in Plato's cave, returns the land of everyday living to enlighten the unenlightened. On arrival, the world shines with the luster of discrimination and consciousness, signified by "ghee." This rc (mantra) can be seen as the transmigrated soul which has not quite yet achieved complete liberation but returns to the world to both continue on its journey to achieve that liberation and also to instruct other souls on the spiritual wealth of heaven.

In the next rc (mantra) the Rishii once again changes perspective. This time, instead of concentrating on the individual soul the Rishii turns his attention to the macrocosm.

RV 1.164.48:

Twelve spokes, one wheel, three axles, who really understand this?
There, three hundred and sixty are placed, firm and steady.

A MODEST INTERPRETATION:

Rishi Dirghatama gazes upwards to explore another aspect of the natural or-der (*rta*), the astrological houses of the zodiac and the world of asterisms.

"Twelve Spokes."

We saw earlier that the number Twelve can represent so many things. In the RgVedic world, there were twelve months. When Prajapati created the world, he united his mind with Speech (vak). Prajapati thereupon placed various Vedic forces in charge of the various sectors of the universe which comprise the zodiac.

We saw earlier that the Rg Veda (RV 2.27.11; 10.72.9) and Satapatha Brahmana (SPB 1.3.1.2, 3) originally established eight Adityas (Astrological Houses), which eventually became twelve. The number twelve will prove to be significant. From the twelve Adityas (astrological houses) arise the twelve months. The number twelve also gives rise to the twelve incarnations of divine ecstacy and union (Soma), based on the meters found in the sama chant. (RV 10.114.5.) While its ultimate meaning is unsure, the likely interpretation is that the zodiac is imbued with divine characteristics.

"Three Axles"

This is another reference to the Three-Dimensional Universe. The three-axeled wheel refers to the three seasons. (AB 2.7, 8, 9, 10, 11, 12, 13.) The one wheel signifies the one year.

"Three Hundred and Sixty Are Placed"

This portion refers to the days of the year.

The Gayatri metre contains eight syllables. (SPB 1.9.1.17; 2.1.4.14, 17; 3.6.2.8; 3.6.4.20, 27; 3.7.1.28; 4.1.1.8; 4.3.2.7; 5.2.1.5; 5.3.3.5; 6.1.3.6, 19; 6.3.1.21; 6.7.1.27; 7.2.1.26; 8.2.3.14.) The eight syllables are increased by a factor of three, because its recitation at the agnistoma is arraigned in triplets. (SSS 2.10.) The product of the padas with the syllables result in passages in which the metre contains twenty-four syllables. (SPB 3.5.1.10; 4.2.4.20, 21; 6.2.1.22.)

In a year there are fifteen nights to a half moon. (SPB 1.3.5.8.) This also produces a factor of twenty-four, which is increased by the nights to a half moon. Given that over the course of a year the gayatri hymn is chanted three hundred and sixty times, supporting what is stated in the Satapatha Brahmana. It is no coincidence, then, that this is the number of days in a Vedic year. The numeral progression is this:

$$24 \times 15 = 360$$

What are we to make of all this? Recall how the construction specifications for the Agnicayana (The Fire Altar) called for three hundred and sixty units. This was representative of the correspondence of the Agnicayana to the days of the year. This rc (mantra) explains how the days of the year were established in the first instance. The establishment of the days and the year, indeed, is indicative of the progression of time, an immutable characteristic of the Vedic dharma (*rta*).

There is an order or sequencing that regulates the movement of physical objects and the sequence in which that movement occurs. *Rta* creates, operates and regulates that movement. *Rta* is the active principle that

- controls the regulation of time and the temporal sequence of everyday life and
- maintains the balance between the cosmic and microcosmic levels.

The goal of the journey of the worshiper in the Vedic path of salvation is to live in harmony with *rta*, its reflection and presence in the universe, and incorporate its precepts in the worshiper's life during the journey to salvation and liberation.

One aspect of *rta*, satya, is that bundle of cosmic laws which determine the sequential movement and order of the material universe. Satya not only represents the universe, but it is the universe, the spatial, sequential movement of the universe in which we all live and breathe. It is for this reason that one of the definitions Williams Monier gives to "satya' is "existence." So, according to the principles of satya, when an automobile moves from point A to point B, all things being equal, the sequence of its movement is out of sequence, non-linear, out of sequential order, akin to the filming style of a Quentin Tarantino movie.

Satya is the active principle that regulates this movement. It is the active principle that allows the automobile to proceed to Point B, by traversing through the seven mid-way point, in a linear, sequential order. Why is this?

Rta is not subject to the rules, laws, and constraints of temporal sequencing. (RV 10.131.3.) If *Rta* regulates the movement and order of the universe, that sequential order could be subject to any one of a number of variations. This is because *Rta* is the master principle of the placement of temporal sequencing. As a cosmic force *rta*, is able to take different forms in different contexts and situations and transform these elements in a working operation. (RV 10.131.4.) This cosmic force permits the multiplicity of universes, because these multiple universes are the products of *rta*'s ability to determine its own temporal and spatial placement in the universe and manifest that temporal and spatial placements differently in different dimensions as reflected in the applicable stage of existence.

Satya, the counterpart of the cosmic order (*rta*), would not have the automobile traveling from Point A to Point B run out of sequence. Without the dynamic force of cosmic order which inheres in *rta*, Satya would not permit our automobile would proceed to Point B in a straight linear line

In the Vedic dharma the Natural Order may impel but it does not compel.

A person's destiny is determined fixed and unalterable in time and space in satyam. (RV 10.131.4.) The divine dynamic order (*rta*) would allow for this traversal, because fundamental differences between *Rta* and satya, as an expansive cosmic order, it is not so fixed and pre-determined. While Satya is the earth-bound passage of time, *Rta* is indeed beyond all space and time. However, according to the temporal sequencing subject to the rules of satyam, on the microcosmic level of a person's fate or destiny, if one event is out of sequence, that person's fate, indeed, the operation of everything in and everyone around that person, is altered. This is the Natural Order of the operation of the material existence, where events are predestined.

Whereas a person's life is more or less predetermined, a modicum of free will exists in Rta. Once the worshiper transcends the mental and physical strictures of the material world, the wider macrocosmic operation of *Rta* control. This is the domain of the Three-Dimensional Universe and beyond. In this realm the worshiper truly takes control not only of the personal life but the immediate surroundings.

The operative rules of Satya (predestination) and *Rta* (freedom) are not mutually exclusive. Both are cast from the same mold and are generated at the same stage of creation. (RV 1.190.1.) It was only in the following stage that time divisions were created by the "movements of the ocean," (RV 1.190.2), a coded reference that time only matters when individual conscious awareness appears in the world. Break free from the fetters of material existence, and achieve mastery over the mind, and one controls the passage of time.

Patanjali recognized this in his Yoga Sutras by stating that accomplished yogis acquire supranatural powers, siddhis, one of which is the ability to break free of the temporal confines. In this state, the limitations of past, present and future become blurred and the yogi is able to essentially travel in time. Mastery of the physical elements when meditating on the outer manifestations, true nature, underlying principle, temporal sequence, and purpose of something. (YS 3.45, 46.) In the yoga of Patanjali, much as in modern physics, the passage of time is simply a component of matter and a truly liberated a yogi will be released from physical, as well as psychological, limitations in the mastery of samadhi. This siddhi, as well as the others, is a feature of the Natural Order.

In much the same way, when focused on the Natural Order the worshiper is liberated. No longer subject to the dichotomous rules of the Two-Dimensional Universe, the worshiper is free to rise above to higher levels of personal spiritual freedom. On a personal level, channeling the universal laws of *Rta* confers the powers of self-determination and personal freedom to the worshiper and serves as a guide-post in the Vedic path to salvation. It is the worshiper's goal to know the Divine Law, *rta*, and incorporate its teachings into the worshiper's life and conduct. (VS, 11:47.) In the same way, once made a part of the worshiper's life, the laws of *Rta* is transformed into the truth of the worshiper's existence — the realm of Satya — and is followed in thought, word and deed. (VS, 11:47.) In a real sense, the laws which power the Vedic dharma transforms the worshiper's life.

RV 1.164.49:

Saraswati is the beast, eternal, receives riches,
and is the giver of nourishment to the entire superior.

A MODEST INTERPRETATION:

The Saraswati is an ancient river. It was once one of the greatest in the Indus Valley, but which has long dried up over, some estimates say, over four thousand years ago. However, the Saraswati, the river, is mentioned many times in the RgVeda, which indicate its antiquity.

Saraswati is also a dynamic Vedic force. As a Vedic force, it primarily represents the Word, Logos.

RV 1.164.50:

The gods perform sacrifice with sacrifice.
They are the first dharma.
They gain the heavenly values.

A MODEST INTERPRETATION:

This rc (mantra) underscores the importance of spiritual rebirth. The rc (mantra) implies that the Vedic forces are the source of the sacrifice. The paradox is that rebirth implies the death of something or someone else.

- Just as Indra is reborn when as the sacrificer he kills Vrtra, so is the worshiper reborn when an offering is made at the sacrifice. (KB 15.3.)
- Just as the Soma plant is "killed" when they are pulverized to make the Soma juice, so does the divine essence of that admixture produce the Vedic principle of Soma, divine union, during the Soma sacrifice. (KB 3.32; SPB 3.2.6.6; 3.9.4.3; 3.9.4.8; 3.9.4.23; 4.3.4.1.)

Similarly, the "killing" of metals is the necessary first step to the rebirth of the metal as a higher form.

- Prajapati in offering and reproducing himself at the sacrifice, saves himself from Death, is re-born, and achieves life eternal. (SPB 2.2.4.7; 2.3.3.2; 3.9.4.17; 11.1.2.1.)

- Indra asked Agni, the Principle of Change, and Brhaspati, to sacrifice him, and they did so. As a result, each was reborn: Indra, as indriyam, articulation; Agni, as tejas, the source of divine energy; and Brhaspati, as brahman, the divine speech. (MS 2.4.6; 43.12.)

- As a result of the animal sacrifice, the sacrificer renews his fires, and thus himself, when he cooks the victim. (SPB 11.7.1.1.)

Prajapati's self-sacrifice sets an example to the worshiper. When Prajapati sacrificed himself at the sacrifice, so too will the worshiper, who lives on with the remaining progeny. (SPB 2.2.4.8.) These examples underscore the importance of sacrifice for spiritual renewal:

- The worshiper is born again through the sacrifice. (RV 10.61.19; 10.101.11.)

- To arrive at this place of personal transformation, the worshiper must have a belly full of Soma. (RV 10.101.11.)

- The worshiper is thereby transformed through yajna to observe and follow the dictates of the divine cosmic order, *rta*, through the tongue of change (Agni). (RV 6.50.2.)

- As a result of being "twice born" the worshiper attains Divine Union (Soma) and becomes one with the God(s) and drinks the milk from the cup of the cosmic order, rta. (RV 10.61.19.)

These passages imply a central truth with regards to the Sacrifice which was explained earlier: There is a give-and-take between the Microcosm (humankind) and the Macrocosm (the universe). This give-and-take is an outgrowth of the binary, dualistic Two-Dimensional Universe. On the one hand, the worshiper seeks and offers obligations to the chosen Vedic force or energy. On the other hand, the force and energy of the chosen Vedic force is channeled to the worshiper. On a rudimentary level, this give-and-take is the bargained for exchange for the condition of life in the universe: One being dies so another may live. The dynamics of the exchange takes many forms and is premised on a fundamental assumption that if it is accurately performed sacrifice has a secret power to produce the desired effect. This give-and-take process is the essence of how the natural order (rta) and how it operates.

The process of being reborn is one aspect of this give and take. It is accomplished through the agency of the Vedic divine dynamic forces at work during the sacrificial rite. (RV 1.148.1.) Where does this rebirth occur? The Svar, subtle region wherein the essence of the cosmic order (*rta*), is the culmination of the give-and-take process of the sacrifice. The capacity or quality of being born again, dvija, is present in these dynamic forces, a quality present primarily in Agni, the principle of change. This aspect of spiritual rebirth inherent in the principle of change is conveyed to the worshiper as well, and the worshiper's soul is transformed, born again, such that he or she has been made a wholly new and different — a purified — person, one conjoined with the cosmos and the divinities. This transformation clearly allows the possibility of the worshiper being spiritually reborn. In its most complete manner this transformation is what is meant by Divine Union; the worshiper shares the qualities of divinities, i.e., immortality. These passages from the Rg Veda are relevant to this issue of divine union and serve as a how-to list for the Vedic dharma.

- The sacrifice subsumes the qualities of the subtle region wherein the essence of the Vedic dharma. (RV 1.148.1.)
- The sacrifice was established when the subtle region wherein the essence of the Vedic dharma was placed in the Vedic cosmos. (RV 5.66.2.)
- These dynamic Vedic forces and forefathers guide the worshiper in the ascent to the region where the essence of dynamic force of cosmic order resides and during the Vedic path to salvation and liberation. (RV 1.71.2.)
- The worshiper seeks access to the region wherein lies the essence of Vedic dharma, the taking aspect of the sacrificial rite. (RV 4.40.2; 5.60.1; 7.90.6.)
- Through the sacrifice and during the journey on the Vedic path to liberation, the worshiper seeks to know the Vedic dharma (*rta*) and its essence (Svar). (RV 10.66.4.)

- The worshiper seeks the assistance of the Duad (Asvins) in the Vedic Path to liberation and to the region where the essence of dynamic force of cosmic order. (RV 8.76.4.)
- The worshiper seeks the truth of the Vedic dharma with the help of the purified mind (Soma)(RV 9.4.2; 9.59.4; 9.61.18; 9.73.1; 9.90.4; 9.98.8), and with the help of the Indra's manifestation as Strength and Grace (RV 6.72.3; 8.3.13), both of which confers the essence of the Vedic dharma (*rta*) to the worshiper.
- The Principle of Change (Agni) confers the essence of the Vedic dharma (*rta*) to the worshiper (RV 2.2.7, 10; 8.48.8), in conjunction with Bala (Indra). (RV 8.48.8.)
- The worshiper ascends to the region where the essence of dynamic force of cosmic order resides through the sama chant. (RV 1.52.9.)
- Once reborn, the worshiper acquires all the attributes of the dynamic, cosmic order: food (immortality), horses (discrimination), and the rays of the essence of the Vedic dharma (*rta*) (knowledge). (RV 4.45.6.)
- Once reborn, awareness (Usas) in the worshiper grows, whether that self-awareness is derivative of the rebirth, or awareness of the worshiper's place in the cosmic order and shines throughout the world. (RV 3.61.4; 7.81.4.)

The lesson of these passages and of the Asyavamasya Sukta is that sacrifice is of divine origin and is part and parcel of *rta*. The very dynamic cosmic order, *rta*, is the result of Agni, the Principle of Change, offering itself to the other dynamic Vedic forces. (RV 3.6.6 - 10.) Sacrifice is its own reward. An act done in the name of self-sacrifice results in the spiritual renewal of the worshiper. It is a necessary element to the perpetual existence of the Vedic dharma (*rta*).

RV 1.164.51:

This water goes up and down on a daily basis.
The Parjanyas enliven the earth;
The fire enlivens the heaven.

A MODEST INTERPRETATION:

"This Water Goes up and down on a Daily Basis."

The interesting feature of this rc (mantra) is the water flowing up and down. This is counter-intuitive, of course, another paradox of water flowing up. (SV, 3.2.3. For waters "flowing down" see RV 1.174.9; 2.33.1; 7.18.15; 9.6.4.) The dynamic Vedic force behind the principle of the Knowledge and Divine Grace, Indra, acting in unison with the attribute of Vital Air, the Asvins, cause the waters to ascend upwards to the mind. (RV 1.32.8.) The true import of this rc, therefore, serves as the basis for and illustrates the upward surging movement of the kundalini serpent as it travels upward along the susumna nadi.

"The Parjanyas Enliven the Earth."

Prajanya is the Vedic deity for the physical phenomenon of rain. This rc (mantra) is a reference to the rain replenishing the earth.

In enlivening the earth, Prajanya recycles the worshiper's soul as well as and in the manner of rain. This process is described in the Five Fires of the Vedas. As you can guess, the Five Fires are part of the Five-Dimensional Universe.

These are the five fires:

- *The Heavenly Fire.*

    Humans are sacrificed at death by cremation, becoming food for the divine Vedic energies and principles and transformed by the heavenly fire into Soma, the purified mind. This fire transforms the human body at death and upon the funeral pyre. The smoke, ciders, and ashes carrying the soul upwards to the heaven. (BU, 6.2.14; Ch.Up., 5.4.1.)

- *The Fire of Parjanya.*

    This fire transforms Soma and the souls in its command into rain. Parjanya is the Vedic divine force for rain. The soul carried upwards to the heavens to be met by Parjanya. (BU, 6.2.10; Ch.Up., 5.5.1; 5.6.1.)

- *The Vegetative Fire.*

    Soma, the divine food, releases the rain, its essence, to earth, where it is transformed into vegetation. Rain is the essence of Soma (Purification), as divine food, falls to the earth with the souls in transmigration. (BU, 6.2.11; Ch.Up., 5.4.2.)

- *The Digestive Fire.*

    When these food plants containing the human should are eaten, they are transformed into seamen by the man-fire, the digestive fire. The rain containing the seeds of the souls in transmigration are transformed to semen and are absorbed by the plant life and fauna and eaten by man or animal. (BU, 6.2.12.)

- *The Female Fire.*

    The semen is transformed into a Purusa, a person, by the woman-fire. The semen is transformed into a Purusa. (BU, 6.6.2.13.)

Food is implicated in this rc (mantra). Food is the by-product of these Fires. The entire Natural Order, in fact, is divided into two parts, the eater and the eaten. (SPB 10.6.2.1.) In the Veda, food, that which is eaten, takes several forms:

- Food is associated with sustenance. (RV 5.70.2.)

- Food is life. (RV 8.3.24.)
- Soma is food. (RV 9.55.2; 9.41.4; 9.61.1, 3; 9.9.63.2; 9.64.13; 9.65.13; 9.66.4, 23, 31; 9.71.8; 9.74.2, 3; 9.85.3; 9.91.5; 9.97.5; 9.99.2; 9.101.11; 9.104. (Soma food of the gods); 10.94.6.)
- Food is associated with wealth. (RV 8.5.36.) It goes without saying that the "wealth" referred to here, nor in any passage from the Vedas mentioning wealth, riches, or the like, is materially wealth. They are the spiritual endowments which are communicated to the worshiper from the Vedic forces and energies.
- Food is also associated with progeny (RV 7.96.6; 9.8.9; 9.13.3; 9.65.21), which, because a person can expect to live on after death through his or her issue, is representative of immortality.
- Water or the waters are considered food. (RV 1.30.1; 1.33.11; 1.52.2; 1.63.8; 1.100.5; 2.34.5; 2.35.1, 11; 2.41.18; 3.4.7; SPB 2.1.1.3; 13.8.1.4, 13.)

In the coded language of the Veda, to say something is food is to refer to the entire universe and all that exists in it. (BU 1.5.1.) Adi Sankara, in his Commentary of this portion of the Brhadaranyakaupanishad, states that this is tantamount to saying that Food is the Object.

Agni (Change and Transformation) is the Eater of Food, both in his physical aspect of fire and in the sacrificial aspect as the fire altar. (SPB 10.6.2.2.) In all aspects, Agni (Change and Transformation) is the Eater of Food. (SPB 2.1.4.28; 2.2.1.1; 2.4.4.1; 8.6.3.5; 10.4.1.11; 11.1.6.9.) As the Eater, Agni produces food again and again. In the process of producing food again and again, the entire Natural Order is created. Being the Eater of Food is coded language for saying that Agni is the Subject, the Absolute Self.

This is not a power reserved only to Vedic deities. All the talk about "conquering death" or "becoming immortal" is coded language signifying that Agni, the principle of Change, transforms the worshiper, who ordinarily an object in the Natural Order, to the Subject. Taking food to a deeper level of abstraction, once transformed into the Eater of food takes the worshiper takes several forms:

- Is complete in Speech. (SPB 3.9.1.9.)

- Stands in the midst of cattle (Knowledge, or food). (SPB 7.5.2.14.)
- Becomes the eater of food during and as a result of the sacrifice. (SPB 1.3.2.11, 12, 14, 15; 1.8.3.5, 6; 4.2.1.9.)
- When the worshiper completes the sacrifice. (SPB 10.3.5.8.)
- The worshiper who fasts at the time of the full moon. (SPB 1.6.3.37.)

The worshiper takes on these characteristics once this aspect of Vedic Dharma, the Natural Order (*rta*) is incorporated into his or her life. But dharma enlightens other aspects.

"The Fire Enlivens the Heaven."

The process of enlivening the earth is a reference to the Five Fires doctrine. The Five Fires is the Vedic precursor to the Hindu concept of reincarnation and transmigration of souls. The Five Fires describe the transmigrational journey as the soul travels from one body to another.

Like smoke wafting upwards, when a person departs from this world, the soul travels upwards in the air. (BU, 5.10.1.) In his commentary of this stanza of the Upanishad, Sankara states that this destination is the hiranyagarbha, the cosmic egg or germ.

Whether the concept of reincarnation was recognized in the Vedic world is a topic of scholarly debate. If this mantra does not settle that debate in favor of recognizing reincarnation, it certainly provides its ideological basis. The cycle of fire can be repeated over and over forever. This entire process is characterized by Fire, but not just the physical fire. Fire is the process of the changes from the Heavenly Fire, to the Fire of Prajanya, the Vegetative Fire, then to Digestive Fire, and finally to the Female Fire. (BU 6.2.14.) Fire, Agni, is essentially the medium of Change and Transformation from one stage to another. To any stage. This fire becomes the basis for any change and transformation, not simply the recycler of souls. This is the essence of dharma, the Natural Order (*rta*).

Some people do not understand this process and do not understand that everything is subject to change and transformation. Heraclitus certainly understood this. So, when a worshiper understands dharma, the Natural Order (*rta*), and incorporates that learning into his or her life, the endless cycle of rebirth and transmigration is broken. The soul gains immortality and perfection, enters the world of the Hiranyagarbha, never to return to the material world again. (BU 6.2.15.)

The next rc (mantra) expands this concept even further.

1.164.52:

The divine bird, the child of the waters,
brings satisfaction in the rainy season.
I invoke Saraswati again and again.

A MODEST INTERPRETATION:

This, the last rc (mantra) of the Sukta, sums up the lessons that are learned from the Natural Order (*rta*). The essential elements of the Vedic dharma, the Natural Order (*rta*) are reduced to the individual components contained in this rc.

"The Divine Bird"

The imagery of this expression harkens to the Agnicayana, which purports to form the outline of a Falcon. The Falcon carries special to the Vedic divine forces and principles, most of which are associated with the Falcon:

- Indra, the divine Vedic force of Articulation and Divine Speech, represents the Falcon. (RV 3.43.7; 4.26.1; 6.46.13; 8.34.9; 8.84.3; 10.146.4, 5.)
- The falcon brings empowering Soma to Indra. (RV 4.26.6, 7; 5.95.9; 8.89.8; 9.48.3; 9.38.4.)
- Soma Pavamana, the highly distilled product of the Soma sacrifice, is indeed compared to a falcon. (RV 9.38.4; 9.61.21; 9.67.14; 9.48.3; 9.68.6; 9.71.6, 9; 9.72.3; 9.77.2; 9.86.24; 9.87.6; 9.96.6.)

- The Maruts are thought of as the "most supreme" falcon. (RV 4.26.4; 8.20.10; 10.37.5.)
- The Asvins, symbol of the Divine Duality of the universe, are associated with the falcon. (RV 5.74.9; 5.78.4; 8.62.4.)
- Mitra-Varuna, dual Vedic forces, are also associated with the falcon. (RV 7.63.5.)
- That most formidable Vedic forces, Agni, the principle of Change and Flux, is the "Falcon of the Sky," ((RV 7.15.4; 10.11.4) and is otherwise compared with the falcon. (RV 4.6.10.)

This comparison segues perfectly with the next portion of this rc (mantra).

"The Child of the Waters."

This is a reference to Agni, the Principle of Change. There is an inextricable connection between the Principle of Change (Agni) and the Waters. This is expressed in many ways:

- A well-known epithet for Agni the Principle of Change is that he is the son of the waters. (RV 1.22.6; 1.122.4; 1.143.1; 1.145.1; 1.186.5; 2.31.6; 2.35.1, 2, 3, 7, 9, 13; 3.9.1; 5.41.10; 6.50.12, 13; 7.34.15; 7.47.2; 10.30.3; 10.92.13.)
- Change (Agni) lives in the waters. (RV 1.65.3, 4, 9, 10; 1.67.3, 4, 9, 10; 170.3, 4; 1.95.4, 5, 8; 1.44.2; 1.149.4; 2.4.2; 3.1.3; 3.72.2; 3.55.12.)
- An entire Sukta, RV 2.35, is devoted to the "Son of Waters," which is the Principle of Change (Agni).
- Change (Agni) was born in the waters. (RV 1.95.4, 5, 8; 3.1.4; 3.5.8.)
- Not only is Agni the child of the waters, but he is carried by the celestial waters. (RV 1.59.4; 1.71.2; 2.35.3.1.4; 9, 14; 9.92.4.)
- Change (Agni) is the "grandson" of the Waters. (RV 1.122.4, 6; 1.143.1; 1.186.5; 2.35.3; 3.9.1; 3.29.11; 5.32.4; 5.41.1; 7.34.15.)
- The active principle of Change (Agni) has been described as the kinsman of the waters (RV 1.65.7, 8) and the germ of the waters

(RV 1.70.3; 1.95.4; 3.5.1), the latter signifying the initial stages of the powers of purification.

- The Principle of Change (Agni) bestows peace through the waters. (AV 2.10.2.)
- The active principles of Change (Agni) produces the waters. (RV 3.4.2.)
- Fire, the essential quality of Change (Agni), protects the water. (AV 11.2.8.)
- The Principle of Change (Agni) is described as the "Bull (vRSabha) of the Standing Waters." (RV 7.5.2; 2.35.13.)

The two principal epithets typifying the evolutionary process of the waters is apaa garbho, seed of the waters:

- Agni is described as the child or the germ of the waters, apaa garbha. (RV 1.70.3; 3.5.3.)
- Agni is born of the waters. (RV 2.1.1.)

The waters are the mothers, the creator, of the universe. (RV 1.95.4; 3.92; 6.50.7; 10.35.2.) The waters thus become the material embodiment of the Principle of Change and Transformation (Agni), the subtle vital creator of the world. (RV 3.1.12, 13.) This Vedic energy is the first principle, essence, and material cause of the visible world.

"Brings Satisfaction in the Rainy Season."

This evolutionary aspect of the Principle of Change (Agni) is furthered in this rc (mantra) by Agni bringing his satisfaction in rain.

"I Invoke Saraswati"

Saraswati is a manifestation of Agni's fire from the firmament. (BD, 3.13.) There is a reason the worshiper invokes Saraswati. Saraswati is divine Vedic force representing Vak, Logos, the First Principle, Paratman. (RV 3.5.15, 16; AV 5.10.8; TB 1.6.2.2; TS 2.1.2.6; AB 3.1.2, 3; KS 10.1.) RV 1.164.45 teaches there are four elements to Vak, and they correspond to the four, broad, dimensions of the multi-universe.

Level of Vak	Corresponding Dimension of the Universe
Vaikhari	Two-Dimensional Universe
Madhyama	Three-Dimensional Universe
Pasyanti	Five-Dimensional Universe
Para	Seven-Dimensional Universe

This is the overview-representation of the Vedic dharma, the Natural Order (*rta*).

- The Natural Order begins at Vaikhari, the underlying basis of material existence present in the Two-Dimensional Universe, where the worshiper experiences the insane tug and pull of maya.
- Beginning to break free of the chains of maya, the worshiper begins to live and experience in the material world reflected in the Three-Dimensional Universe.
- Through meditation the worshiper discovers the subtle basis of the material world in the Five-Dimensional Universe.
- Through intense worship, ritual and meditation (tapas) the worshiper, if lucky, transcends to the liberation of the Seven-Dimensional Universe. Salvation has been achieved.

This final entry represents the final destination for the worshiper.

Life is a journey, and every journey has a destination. In the Vedic world, that destination is the Seven-Dimensional Universe. The Vedas have many names for this destination spot. It is called Rodasi, heaven, the transcendent realm of divinity, the world of the gods, nirvana, the Atman, and many others. It is both the source of the worshiper's soul and its destination. When the worshiper's soul finally arrives to the Seven-Dimensional Universe, it gets back to the place where it once began its journey. It is here that the worshiper's soul belongs. When the Brahmanas speak of re-integrating the body to Prajapati, this is coded language to signify uniting with the Vedic dharma, the Natural Order (*rta*). The full import of the Vedic dharma is found in the very beginning of this book when it was said that enlightenment and understanding obtained when the worshiper lives its life in accordance with the Natural Order (*rta*). The task of the Vedic worshiper is to know and understand the surrounding dharma and implement the vital forces and rhythms in life. Much later, in his Divine Comedy, Dante would describe the arrival of his soul as joining with the love that moves the stars. Living in accordance with the Vedic dharma is comparable. There, the worshiper's journey is complete, at least for the moment, at least for this lifetime. If there are no more lessons to learn, the soul is liberated and dwells for eternity with the Absolute Self, at peace. If not, the soul gets ready for the next journey and will try again.

APPENDIX: PRINCIPLE VEDIC FORCES IN THE DHARMA

Call them the Vedic deities if you want, but these deities, and others, represent active material and subtle forces and principles which operate continuously in the Vedic dharma. A short list of the principal Vedic deities, and the forces they represent, are the following:

Agni, the Principle of Transformation.

Indra, the Principle of Increase, which subsumes several other vital forces:

- Conjunction and Unity.
- Strength and Force.
- Maker of Forms.
- Articulation of Mind and Matter.
- Pure Energy Light.
- Force of Mind, Consciousness, and Discernment.

Soma, the Principle of Bliss, Purification, and Spiritual Ecstasy.
Vayu, the Principle of the Vital Life Force.
Brhaspati, the Principle of Consciousness.
Savitr, Principle of the Perpetuality of Creation.
Varuna, the Principle of *rta*, the Vedic dharma, the dynamic, cosmic, Natural Order.
Pusan, Principle of Direction and Pathways.
Asvins, Principle of Duality.

ABBREVIATIONS

AA	Aitatreya Aranyaka
AB	Aitatreya Brahmana
ASSu	Asvalayana SrautaSutra
ASG	Asvalayana Ghrya Sutra
AV	Atharva Veda
BG	Bhavagad Gita
BD	Brhad Devata
Br.S.	Brhat Samhita
BAU	Brhad Aranyaka Upanishad
CU	Chandogya Upanishad
GB	Gopatha Brahmana
JB	Jaiminiya Brahmana
JUB	Jaiminiya Upanishad Brahmana
KA	Katha Aranyaka
KB	Kaustika Brahmana
KGS	Kathaka Ghyra Samhita
KS	Kathaka Samhita

MB	Mahabharata
MS	Maitrayani Samhita
Nir.	Nirukta
R	Rasadhyaya
RV	Rg Veda
RV-K	Khila Sutras of the Rg Veda
SA	Sakhaya Aranyaka
SB	Sadvimsa Brahmana
SBP	Sri Bhagavatam Purana
SK	Sankhya Karika
SPB	Satapatha Brahmana
SSS	Sakhayana Srautasutra
SV	Sama Veda
TA	Tattiritya Aranyaka
TB	Tattiriya Brahmana
TOBV	Tattiriyopanishadbhasyavartikm
TS	Tattiriya Samhita
VBT	Vijnana Bhairava Tantra
VS	Vajasaneyi Samhita
VeS	Vaisesika Sutras
Vas.	Vasistha Samhita
YS	Yoga Sutras
YV	Yajur Veda

Printed in the United States
By Bookmasters